Scribble Scrabble

Ready-in-a-Minute Math Games

Richard M. Sharp

Professor of Education
California State University, Northridge

Vicki F. Sharp

Professor of Education
California State University, Northridge

Seymour Metzner

Professor Emeritus
California State University, Northridge

Illustrations by
Steve Hoeft

[handwritten notes: "Use in Activity Books", "Money Back Sponsorship", "Game Books", "ideal", "1 math game per issue – 36", "1 math game 1 word game per issue"]

TAB Books
Division of McGraw-Hill, Inc.
New York San Francisco Washington, D.C. Auckland Bogotá Caracas Lisbon London Madrid
Mexico City Milan Montreal New Delhi San Juan Singapore Sydney Tokyo Toronto

© 1995 by McGraw-Hill, Inc..
Published by TAB Books, a division of McGraw-Hill, Inc.

Previously published as *Ready-in-a-Minute Math Games* by Prentice-Hall Learning Systems, Inc., © 1975

 This book is printed on recycled paper containing a minimum of 50% total recycled fiber with 15% postconsumer de-inked fiber.

pbk 1 2 3 4 5 6 7 8 9 BBC/BBC 9 9 8 7 6 5

Product or brand names used in this book may be trade names or trademarks. Where we believe that there may be proprietary claims to such trade names or trademarks, the name has been used with an initial capital or it has been capitalized in the style used by the name claimant. Regardless of the capitalization used, all such names have been used in an editorial manner without any intent to convey endorsement of or other affiliation with the name claimant. Neither the author nor the publisher intends to express any judgment as to the validity or legal status of any such proprietary claims.

Library of Congress Cataloging-in-Publication Data
Sharp, Richard M.
    Scribble scrabble : ready-in-a-minute math games / by Richard M.
Sharp, Vicki F. Sharp, Seymour Metzner.
    p.   cm.
    ISBN 0-07-057110-4 (pbk.)
    1. Games in mathematics education.   2. Mathematics—Study and
teaching (Elementary) I. Sharp, Vicki F. II. Metzner, Seymour.
III. Title.
QA135.5.S476 1995
372.7'044—dc20   94-48315
                                                            CIP

Acquisitions editor: Kimberly Tabor
Editorial team: Susan W. Kagey, Editor
                Joanne Slike, Executive Editor
Production team: Katherine G. Brown, Director
                Ollie Harmon, Coding
                Jan Fisher, Desktop Operator
                Nancy K. Mickley, Proofreading
Design team: Jaclyn J. Boone, Designer   SS1
                Kathryn Stefanski, Associate Designer   0571104

Contents

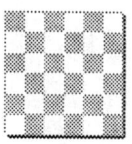

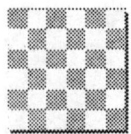

Introduction for Parents and Teachers

What distinguishes children who are successfully learning mathematics from those who are having difficulties? Parents and teachers are not the only ones interested in the answer. Various federal, state, and local governments have spent millions of dollars sponsoring research to uncover the secrets of mathematical competence. They recognize that in an increasingly technological and globally competitive world, an educated work force is necessary for a vibrant American economy.

Math research has discovered two elements that are consistently linked to student achievement. One is parental involvement; the other is teacher use of manipulative materials.

Educational psychologists have long recognized that well-planned instruction involving all the senses and physical activity promotes self-discovery of math concepts and ensures greater retention.

The type of parental involvement most needed is engaging in learning activities with your child. This involvement indicates to your child, far more than words of encouragement, the importance of this assignment.

The activities and gameboards in this book present important skills and concepts in a motivational game format adapted to one-on-one instruction. Important material that has often been presented as dull, repetitive exercises now becomes challenging and appealing. The interaction with another person, particularly a parent, adds tremendous zest to the activity. A further benefit is that these gameboards require only minimal language skills.

We strongly suggest, particularly in the cases of younger or easily discouraged children, that the student initially experience the maximum possible degree of success. Achieving this goal might well require "throwing" a few games, but we're sure it comes under the heading of a forgivable sin done for a good cause.

Super-reluctant learners might be enticed into playing these games with some form of reward structure—perhaps edible goodies or a particularly prized privilege. Once the child is "hooked" in the pleasure of the activity itself, the reward incentive can be discontinued.

We are sure parents and teachers will enjoy these activities every bit as much as the children.

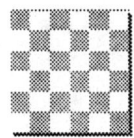

Teaching Suggestions

This book offers a rich assortment of spinner, matrix, and card learning games. The concepts and skills range from whole number operations to geometry. The directions and materials are simple, and all the games are readily reproducible. Furthermore, they have a wide variety of classroom uses and are adaptable to varying instructional objectives.

Group Size

These math learning games are designed to be used as flexibly as possible. They may be used in learning centers, small group instruction, one-on-one tutorial situations, or with a whole class. The gameboards can be enlarged to chart size (18" × 24") for use with a large group of children. Although the directions for each game call for two players, a team of two or more players may act as partners against another team of comparable size. A game may involve three players with one player acting as the group leader who has a gameboard with the correct answers.

Materials

The materials required for any of the games are ordinary school supplies. You'll need paper, pencils, crayons, paper clips, scissors, dice, toothpicks, and markers (beans, disks, chips, and so on). Inexpensive calculators are helpful in doing long and tedious work. All the gameboards should be duplicated on copy machines so that the originals can be used again.

Introducing a Game

❶ The teacher or parent should read through the directions completely and see the strategy for each game before explaining it to an individual child or to the class.

❷ Playing a practice, "get-acquainted" game before playing for a score is a good idea. Play a practice game right after you explain the directions.

❸ As soon as the children understand what to do, allow them to play independently with a partner.

Modifying a Gameboard

The games may be further adapted to specific class or individual needs by using self-adhesive blank labels and then making a transparency or master from this new gameboard.

SPINNING DUET

Spinning Duet

Objective

✸ Add two-digit numbers, with and without regrouping in the tens' place.

Directions

❶ Two players share the same "Spinning Duet" gameboard.

❷ One player has dark-colored beans or other markers; the other has light-colored beans or markers. The purpose of the game is to get three beans or markers in a line diagonally, horizontally, or vertically.

❸ Player A goes first. First the player spins the two spinners (see "Creating a Spinner" at the end of the instructions) and decides where to place his or her beans on the gameboard. The player may place beans on the two numbers on the spinners or on their sum. For example, if one spinner stops on 18 and the other on 22, the player may decide to place one bean on ⬡18 and another bean ⬡22 or to place one bean on ⬡40 (the sum of 18 and 22).

❹ Player B now takes a turn spinning the two spinners and placing the beans.

❺ Only one bean may be placed on each octagon. A player loses his or her turn when the octagons are covered or when he or she adds incorrectly.

❻ The winner is the first player who places three beans in a line diagonally, horizontally, or vertically.

Creating a Spinner

You'll need a paper clip and a pencil.

❶ Place one end of the paper clip over the dot on the number wheel.

❷ Place the pencil point inside the paper clip on the dot.

❸ Hold the pencil firmly in place and flick the paper clip with your finger so it spins around the pencil.

❹ When the paper clip stops spinning, its tip will indicate your number.

PICK, PLACE, WIN

Pick, Place, Win

Objective

✳ Practice single and multidigit column addition involving patterns.

Directions

❶ Two players share the same gameboard. One uses a bundle of 10 red toothpicks, the other a bundle of 10 blue toothpicks. Each toothpick is 2½" long. Flat plastic toothpicks work best; however, you can use wooden toothpicks if you dip the ends in food coloring so that each player has a different color.

❷ In turn, each player places one toothpick on the gameboard so that it touches as many hexagons as possible. In the following example (from directly beneath the ⟨2⟩ in the top row), the toothpick touches five shapes.

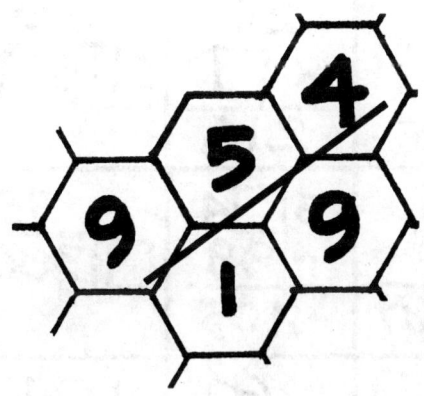

The player adds together the numbers in the hexagons. For this example, the player adds 9 + 5 + 4 + 1 + 9 for a score of 28. (The players may use a calculator.)

Note: Since the gameboard can be enlarged to any size when it is photocopied, the toothpicks will not always cover the same number of hexagons as in the example. To avoid confusion, check how many hexagons a toothpick covers on the gameboard before explaining the game to younger children.

❸ After each turn, the player records his or her score, keeping a running total on scratch paper. No part of any hexagon may be covered more than once and no toothpick may cross another. If the gameboard will not be reused, you might want to cross off the hexagons once they are used.

❹ If a player gives the incorrect sum, he or she scores no points for that turn and loses one toothpick.

❺ The game ends when neither player can place a toothpick on the gameboard. A player's final score is the total of the numbers in the hexagons covered by his or her toothpicks. The highest score wins.

FIX IT

□8 +69 147	73 3)21□	700 −□97 3	102 4)4□8	24 +□7 71
□9 ×3 207	1□4 −98 6	49 □)196	□8 ×3 234	459 +475 □34
591 +□82 1,073	5 □ +8 20	24 ×□ 216	93 2)18□	900 −492 4□8
867 −4□8 369	81 ×7 5□7	3□4 −99 205	95 □)380	23 ×9 20□
72 ×7 5□4	37□ −86 288	260 +6□0 930	104 −□8 6	9 5 +□ 20

PLAYER A

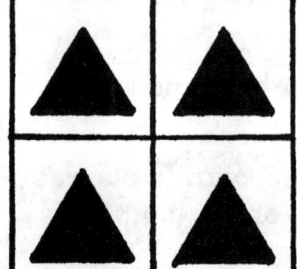

PLAYER B

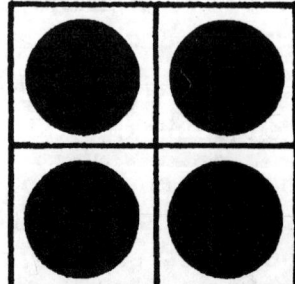

Fix It

Objective

✳ Use the place-holder concept in solving a number operation for addition, subtraction, multiplication, or division.

Directions

❶ Two players share the same gameboard. The missing number (box) in each problem is either a 0, 4, 6, 7, or 9.

❷ Player A cuts out and uses the four squares with the triangles in them, while Player B cuts out and uses the four squares with the circles in them. The players may use other markers; each player needs four markers.

❸ Player A spins (see "Creating a Spinner" at the end of the instructions). If Player A first spins 9, he or she then places a marker over a box containing a problem that can be solved by inserting the number 9. If Player B spins 7, he or she places a marker over a box containing a problem that can be solved by inserting the number 7.

❹ If a player completes a problem incorrectly, he or she loses a turn.

❺ When the players have no markers left, they may shift one of their own markers on the gameboard to a new position.

❻ The players take turns until one player has *three* markers in a straight line diagonally, horizontally, or vertically. That player is the winner.

Creating a Spinner

You'll need a paper clip and a pencil.

❶ Place one end of the paper clip over the dot on the number wheel.

❷ Place the pencil point inside the paper clip on the dot.

❸ Hold the pencil firmly in place and flick the paper clip with your finger so it spins around the pencil.

❹ When the paper clip stops spinning, its tip will indicate your number.

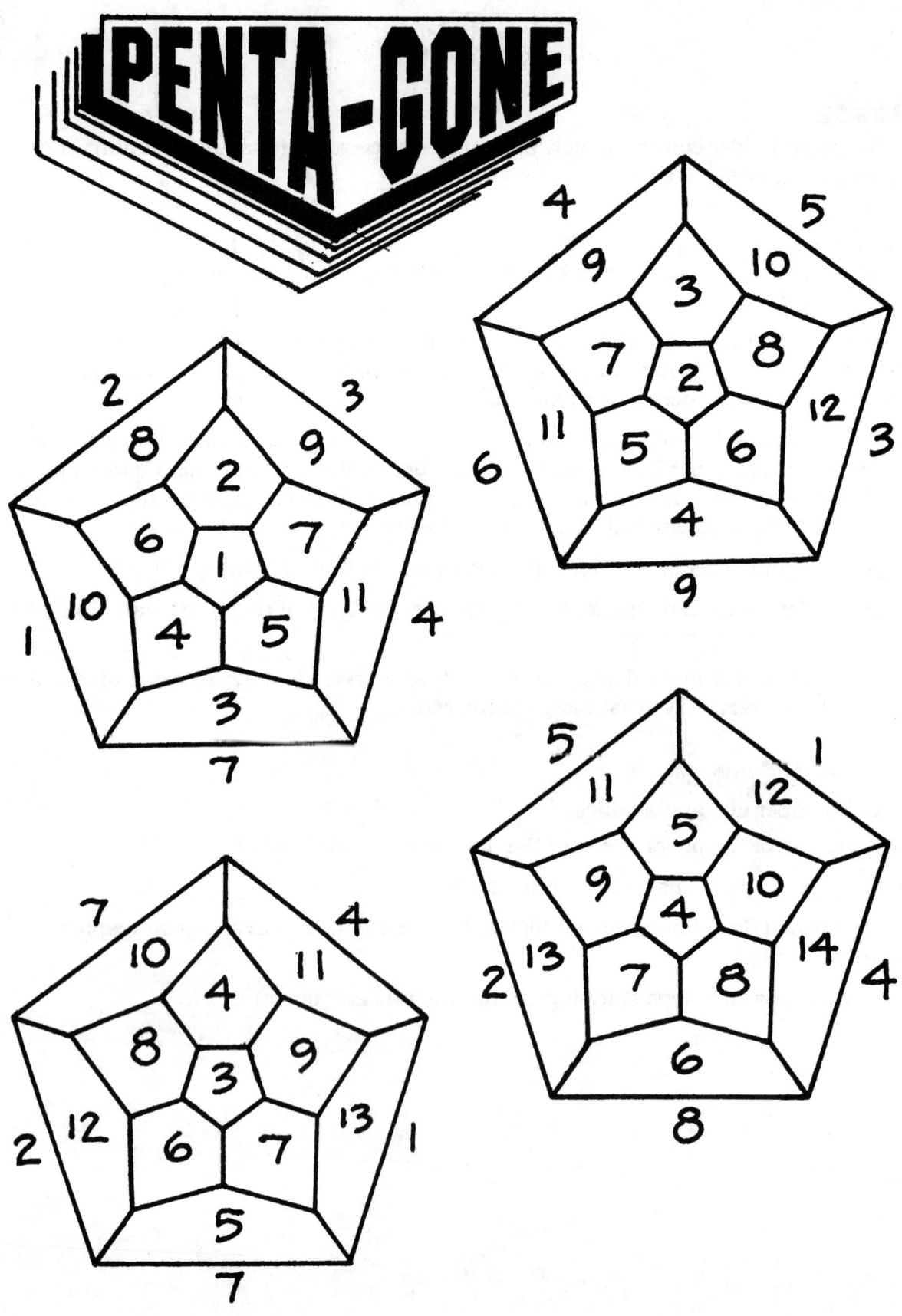

Penta-Gone

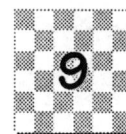

use counters

Objective

✸ Perform multiplication and multidigit addition involving unseen sums and regrouping.

Directions

❶ Two players share the same gameboard. One player uses a red crayon, the other a blue one.

❷ In turn, each player colors over one straight line in the first large pentagon. Before actually choosing a line to color, a player must give the correct product of the two numbers on either side of the line. For example, if a player wants to color the line between 9 and 2, he or she must say "18." The player may trace any uncolored line that is inside or around the large pentagon.

❸ Whenever a player colors three sides of any smaller pentagon (or box) inside the large pentagon, the number inside that box belongs to that player and he or she circles that number with his or her crayon.

❹ Play continues until each number inside the large pentagon is circled. The players then add together their circled numbers. The player with the highest total wins that pentagon.

❺ Players take turns starting each large pentagon.

❻ The player who wins three large pentagons wins the game. If the players tie—they each win two large pentagons—the player with the highest total score of circled numbers wins the game.

Variation

In step 2, younger players may add the two numbers on either side of the line instead of multiplying them. The game continues as usual, following steps 2 through 6 in the directions. If the players cannot find the sum of three or more numbers as instructed in step 4, they can instead count their circled numbers. The player with the highest number wins that pentagon.

PF.

Yr. 4

BLOCK 'EM

45	7	14	24	16	10
54	20	15	5	28	9
64	35	8	12	25	40
49	4	42	30	48	6
60	36	18	32	27	21
8	70	64	72	56	63

(1) (2) (3) (4) (5) (6)

(7) (8) (9) (1) (2) (3)

(4) (5) (6) (7) (8) (9)

(10) (12) (14) (15) (16) (18)

(20) (21) (24) (25) (27) (28)

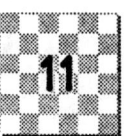

Block 'Em

Objective

✴ Reinforce multiplication of one- and two-digit numbers.

Directions

❶ The players share the same gameboard and two paper clips.

❷ One player uses light-colored beans, the other dark-colored beans. Other markers may be substituted for beans.

❸ Player A places one paper clip on any circled number and the other paper clip on another circled number. Player A multiplies these two numbers together. For example, Player A places one paper clip on the ③ at the end of the second row and the other on the ⑦ in the third row, multiplying 3 and 7 for a product of 21.

❹ Player A then puts a bean or marker on the square containing the product, which, in this example, is in the fifth row and sixth column of the gameboard.

❺ Player B now moves one of the paper clips to another circled number, multiplies the two numbers, and covers this new product with a bean.

❻ The players take turns, moving only one paper clip on each turn.

❼ A player loses a turn if the product is already covered or if the product is not on the gameboard.

❽ Play continues until four neighboring numbers (products) are covered horizontally, vertically, diagonally, or in a square.

❾ The player who first places four beans in a winning position wins the game.

Matchmaker

7	4	8	3	6	9
4	5	6	7	8	9
2	1	5	$35 \div 5$	$36 \div 9$	$24 \div 3$
$36 \div 6$	$81 \div 9$	$32 \div 8$	$40 \div 8$	$42 \div 6$	$72 \div 9$
$63 \div 7$	$18 \div 9$	$12 \div 12$	$45 \div 9$	$27 \div 9$	$54 \div 9$

Matchmaker

Objective

✳ Calculate the quotient in one-step division with no remainders.

Directions

❶ Each player receives a gameboard. Both players cut out the 30 cards on their gameboards.

❷ All the cards (a total of 60) are shuffled together. Each player takes five cards; the remaining cards are placed facedown in a central pile. The top card is turned faceup next to the central pile. Neither player sees the other's cards.

❸ Player A goes first, either by taking the card turned faceup or by drawing a card from the top of the central pile. If the drawn card matches a card in his or her hand, the player places the pair aside, out of play. The player is attempting to match a problem with an answer. For example, Player A matches $\boxed{36 \div 9}$ with $\boxed{4}$ and places this pair of cards aside. Player A then discards a card, placing it face up beside the central pile. In order to make a match, Player B now either takes a card from the discard pile or draws a card from the central pile.

❹ A player may take any card in the discard pile, providing he or she takes all the cards above it, too.

❺ If a player makes a mismatch, he or she returns the drawn card to the bottom of the central pile and loses a turn.

❻ Players continue matching cards until one player has no cards left or until no cards are left in the central pile. The player who goes out first gets a bonus score of five points.

❼ Each player scores one point for each pair of cards matched correctly.

❽ The player who has the most points wins.

SCRIBBLE
CRABBLE

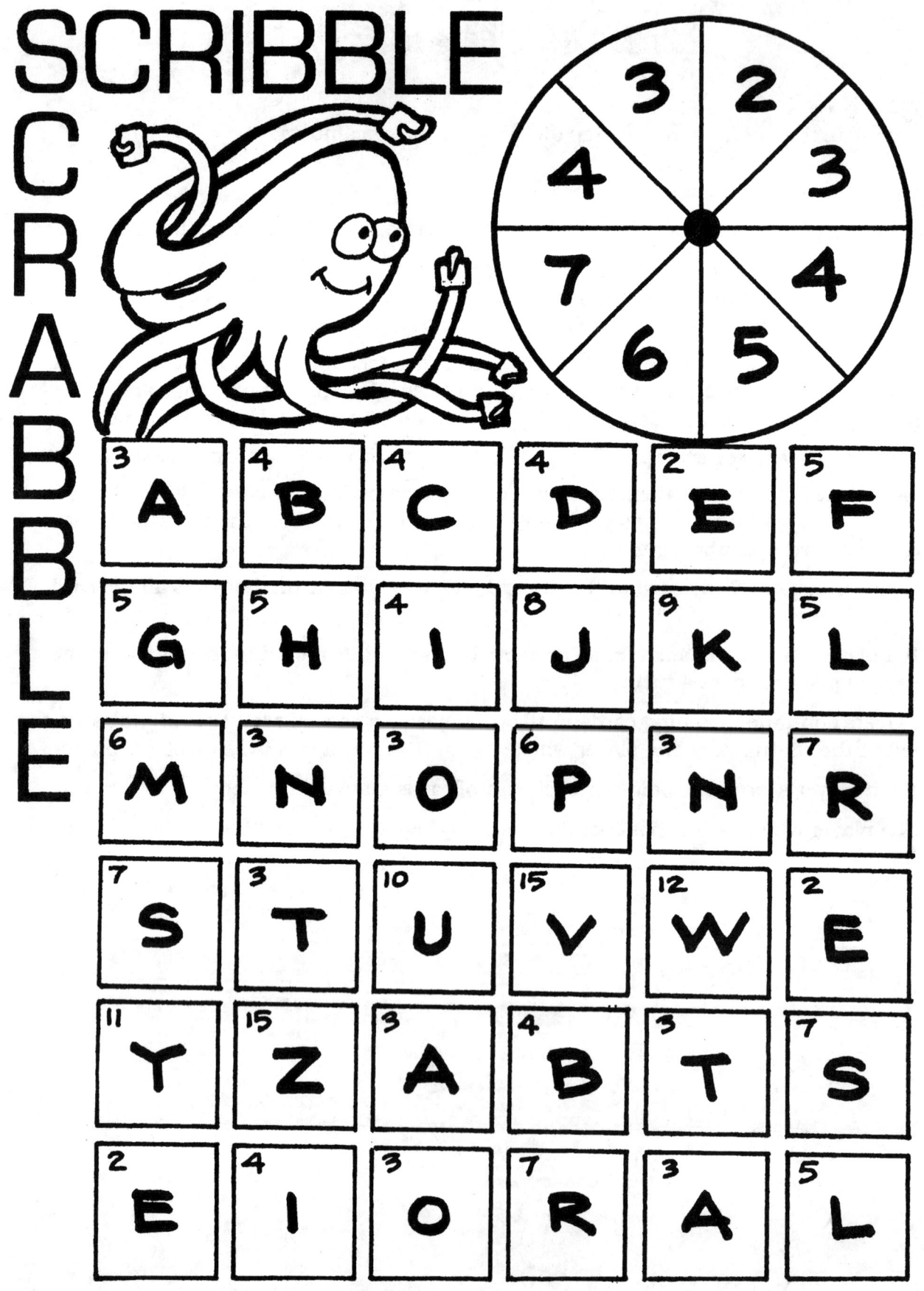

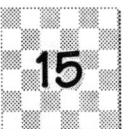

Scribble Scrabble

Objective

✻ Apply the commutative (order) and associative (regrouping) properties for multidigit addition.

Directions

❶ Two players share the same "Scribble Scrabble" gameboard. One player cuts out the 36 alphabet cards and places them face up on the table.

❷ Each player takes a turn spinning a number (see "Creating a Spinner" at the end of the instructions). The number determines the number of cards the players must use to form words. (If the spinner stops on a line, use the higher number.) For example, Player A spins a 3 and then searches for three cards that form a word. He or she combines $\boxed{^5H}\,\boxed{^3A}\,\boxed{^3T}$ to make the word "HAT" and then adds the numbers found in the upper-left-hand corners of the letter cards, 5 + 3 + 3, and records their sum, 11.

❸ Player B, using the remaining cards, tries to find three cards that form a three letter word other than "HAT." If Player B combines $\boxed{^{15}Z}\,\boxed{^3O}\,\boxed{^3O}$, making the word "ZOO," he or she adds 15 + 3 + 3 and records their sum, 21. Both players then return the cards to the table for replay. Player B now spins a number, and the game continues.

❹ If a player is unable to make a word, he or she scores no points for that spin.

❺ The game continues in this manner until one player has scored 100 points or more.

Creating a Spinner

You'll need a paper clip and a pencil.

❶ Place one end of the paper clip over the dot on the number wheel.

❷ Place the pencil point inside the paper clip on the dot.

❸ Hold the pencil firmly in place and flick the paper clip with your finger so it spins around the pencil.

❹ When the paper clip stops spinning, its tip will indicate your number.

CRAZY QUILT

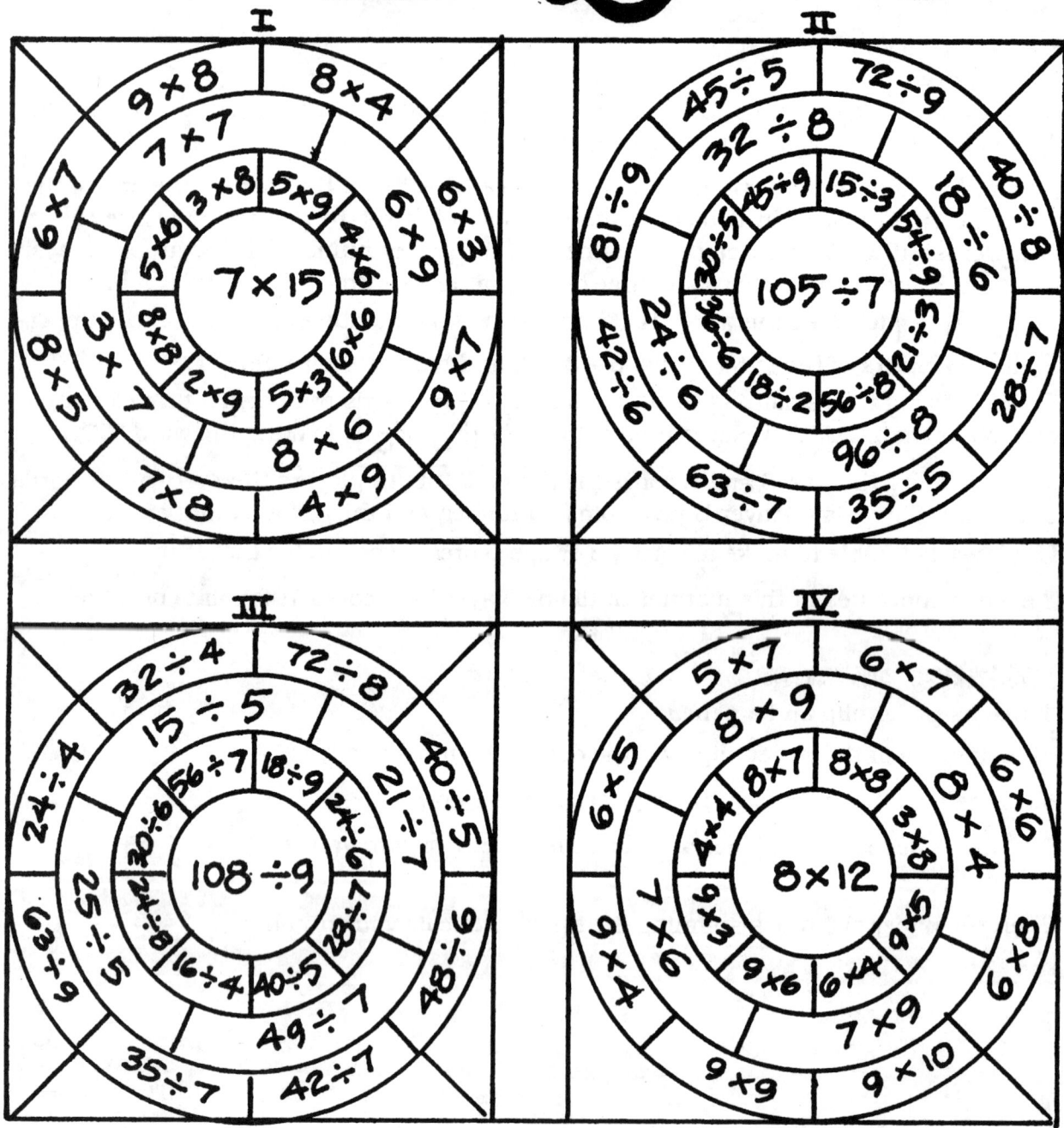

I

- 9 × 8
- 8 × 4
- 7 × 7
- 6 × 7
- 6 × 3
- 6 × 9
- 3 × 8
- 5 × 9
- 5 × 6
- 4 × 6
- 7 × 15
- 8 × 8
- 6 × 6
- 2 × 9
- 5 × 3
- 8 × 5
- 3 × 7
- 9 × 7
- 7 × 8
- 8 × 6
- 4 × 9

II

- 45 ÷ 5
- 72 ÷ 9
- 32 ÷ 8
- 81 ÷ 9
- 40 ÷ 8
- 18 ÷ 6
- 45 ÷ 9
- 15 ÷ 3
- 20 ÷ 5
- 36 ÷ 6
- 54 ÷ 9
- 105 ÷ 7
- 24 ÷ 6
- 21 ÷ 3
- 42 ÷ 6
- 18 ÷ 2
- 56 ÷ 8
- 28 ÷ 7
- 63 ÷ 7
- 96 ÷ 8
- 35 ÷ 5

III

- 32 ÷ 4
- 72 ÷ 8
- 15 ÷ 5
- 24 ÷ 4
- 40 ÷ 5
- 56 ÷ 7
- 18 ÷ 9
- 30 ÷ 6
- 24 ÷ 6
- 21 ÷ 7
- 108 ÷ 9
- 24 ÷ 8
- 28 ÷ 7
- 25 ÷ 5
- 16 ÷ 4
- 40 ÷ 5
- 48 ÷ 6
- 63 ÷ 9
- 49 ÷ 7
- 35 ÷ 7
- 42 ÷ 7

IV

- 5 × 7
- 6 × 7
- 8 × 9
- 6 × 5
- 6 × 6
- 8 × 4
- 4 × 4
- 8 × 7
- 8 × 8
- 3 × 8
- 8 × 12
- 9 × 3
- 3 × 8
- 9 × 5
- 7 × 6
- 9 × 6
- 6 × 4
- 9 × 4
- 6 × 8
- 7 × 9
- 9 × 9
- 9 × 10

Crazy Quilt

Objectives

✹ Multiply two one-digit numbers or divide a two-digit number by a one-digit number with no remainders.

✹ Use color patterns in creating winning strategies.

Directions

❶ Two players use one gameboard. The players share four crayons (for example, red, blue, yellow, and black).

❷ The game starts with Wheel I. The first player picks a problem in that wheel and solves it. If the player solves the problem correctly, he or she colors in that block on the wheel. For instance, if a player chooses 7 × 8, he or she calls out the problem 7 × 8 and its answer, 56, before coloring in that section of the wheel. If the player calls out the wrong answer, he or she loses a turn to color. Next, the other player chooses a problem on that same wheel. Players take their turns on the same wheel until that wheel is won.

❸ A player wins the wheel if he or she is the last one to be able to color a section with a different color from any touching section. The players do not have to color every section in the wheel.

❹ Touching sections may not have the same color.

❺ Play continues until all four wheels have been used.

❻ The player who wins three wheels wins the game. If both players win two wheels, the game is a tie.

BUYER BEWARE !

Buyer Beware

Objective
✳ Add a series of numbers to complete an equation using missing addends.

Directions

❶ Two players share the same gameboard. One player cuts out the nine picture cards in the market basket, while the other player cuts out the 18 number cards at the bottom of the gameboard.

❷ The number cards are shuffled and placed facedown in one pile, while the picture cards are shuffled and placed faceup in another pile.

❸ The players use the number cards as money and try to reach the price on the top picture card. In turn, each player draws a card from the number pile and holds it so that the other player cannot see it. This number card becomes part of the total price each player is trying to reach.

❹ Play continues until both players have decided to stop taking number cards or until one player goes over the price. One player may decide to keep taking number cards although the other has decided to stop. A player who stops must not let the other player know that she or he went over the price until the other player stops too.

❺ Once play has stopped, the player whose number cards add up to a sum closer to the price on the picture card without going over wins the picture card. If the total of a player's number cards goes over the price, the other player wins that picture card. If both players' cards go over the price or there is a tie, neither player wins the picture card, and it is returned to the bottom of the pile for replay.

❻ Before bidding starts on a new picture card, the players collect all the number cards, reshuffle, and place them facedown in a pile.

❼ The player who wins five picture cards first wins the game.

Variation

In step 7, instead of play ending when one player has five picture cards, play continues until all the picture cards are taken. The players add the prices on the picture cards to get their total scores. (The players may use a calculator.) The player with the highest total wins.

Use Coins i Yr1.?
re Reprint.

Phil
Yr 2 game with coins
from supermarket game.

Bombs Away

✓ 1/R3

Objective

✱ Reinforce regrouping skills in multidigit addition and subtraction.

Directions

❶ The players share the same gameboard. One player uses 10 small light-colored beans or other markers; the other player uses 10 small dark-colored beans or other markers.

❷ Holding the 10 beans in their fists, the players take turns dropping the beans anywhere on the gameboard. Each player releases his or her beans all at once from any height.

❸ Counting only one bean for each space, the player adds the numbers in the triangles where the beans fell. If a bean fell on more than one space, the player takes the larger number. Players do not receive any score for beans that do not land on the gameboard.

❹ After both players have dropped their beans and added their scores, the players then subtract the smaller sum from the largest. The player whose number was larger gets the difference as his or her score. If the sums were the same, neither player gets a score for that drop.

❺ A player gets no score if he or she adds incorrectly.

❻ After each drop, the players clear all their beans and reuse them in the next turn.

❼ After 10 drops, the players add their total scores. (The players may use a calculator.) The player with the highest total wins.

PF

SEESAW

44	7	20	9	45	14	50	27	36	63
32	27	12	60	5	4	49	81	18	10
100	14	6	40	70	35	48	30	21	3
72	8	12	24	64	55	40	8	15	120
10	3	6	12	20	24	9	42	54	36
12	5	2	18	60	7	21	40	28	42
56	48	16	10	4	63	15	80	20	12
80	6	45	70	22	33	18	8	32	50
66	12	24	90	36	6	16	77	48	88
10	35	24	16	8	25	20	84	10	96
2	28	30	110	108	40	72	99	60	30
9	36	4	18	54	30	24	72	56	90

÷ ② ③ ④ ⑤ ⑥ ⑦ ⑧ ⑨ ⑩

Seesaw

Yes
Division

Objectives

✶ Use single-digit divisors with no remainders.

✶ Generalize and test rules for divisibility.

Directions

❶ Two players share the gameboard.

❷ Player A uses a red crayon; Player B uses a blue crayon.

❸ Player A chooses a divisor from the row of circles at the bottom of the gameboard. He or she then tries to find a number on the gameboard that divides evenly by that divisor. The player must call out the answer of the problem and then color in the box. For example, the player may choose 4 as the divisor. He or she finds $\boxed{8}$, calls out the answer, 2, and colors the box $\boxed{8}$. Using the *same divisor*, Player B finds a number, calls out its answer, and colors in the number box.

❹ Player B then chooses a divisor to be used by both players. She or he may use the same or another divisor. The players attempt to color four boxes in a line horizontally, vertically, or diagonally with their own color.

❺ Players take turns choosing divisors.

❻ If a player makes an error, he or she loses a turn.

❼ The player who first colors four boxes in a straight line horizontally, vertically, or diagonally wins the game.

Adapt to multiplication. Yr 4

Use counters of different colour

SQUARE DEAL

8×9	54÷6	18+7	23−8	96÷2
19+8	33−6	72÷2	7×5	72÷8
36÷3	6×8	45÷9	37+6	43−9
56÷7	28+5	51−2	51÷3	7×9
21−9	96÷3	3×8	36÷4	19+12

Square Deal

Objectives

✳ Perform one operation involving a basic fact in either addition, subtraction, multiplication, or division.

✳ Develop a winning strategy in a five-by-five matrix (grid).

Directions

❶ Two players share the gameboard.

❷ Starting at any black square (▓) on the gameboard, Player A connects it to a neighboring black square with a horizontal or vertical line. Player B then connects any two neighboring black squares. Diagonal lines are not allowed.

❸ The players may connect two neighboring black squares *anywhere* on the gameboard.

❹ Connecting black squares continues until one player completes a square. The player completing the square receives one point if he or she is able to give the answer to the problem inside that newly completed square. The player then places his or her initials inside that completed square.

❺ If the player is unable to answer the problem correctly, the other player has a chance to give the correct answer and place his or her initials in the square and receive the point.

❻ Play ends when all 25 squares are completed.

❼ The player who has scored the most points wins.

Drag answers onto
square — if correct
reveals letters that
spell out a message.

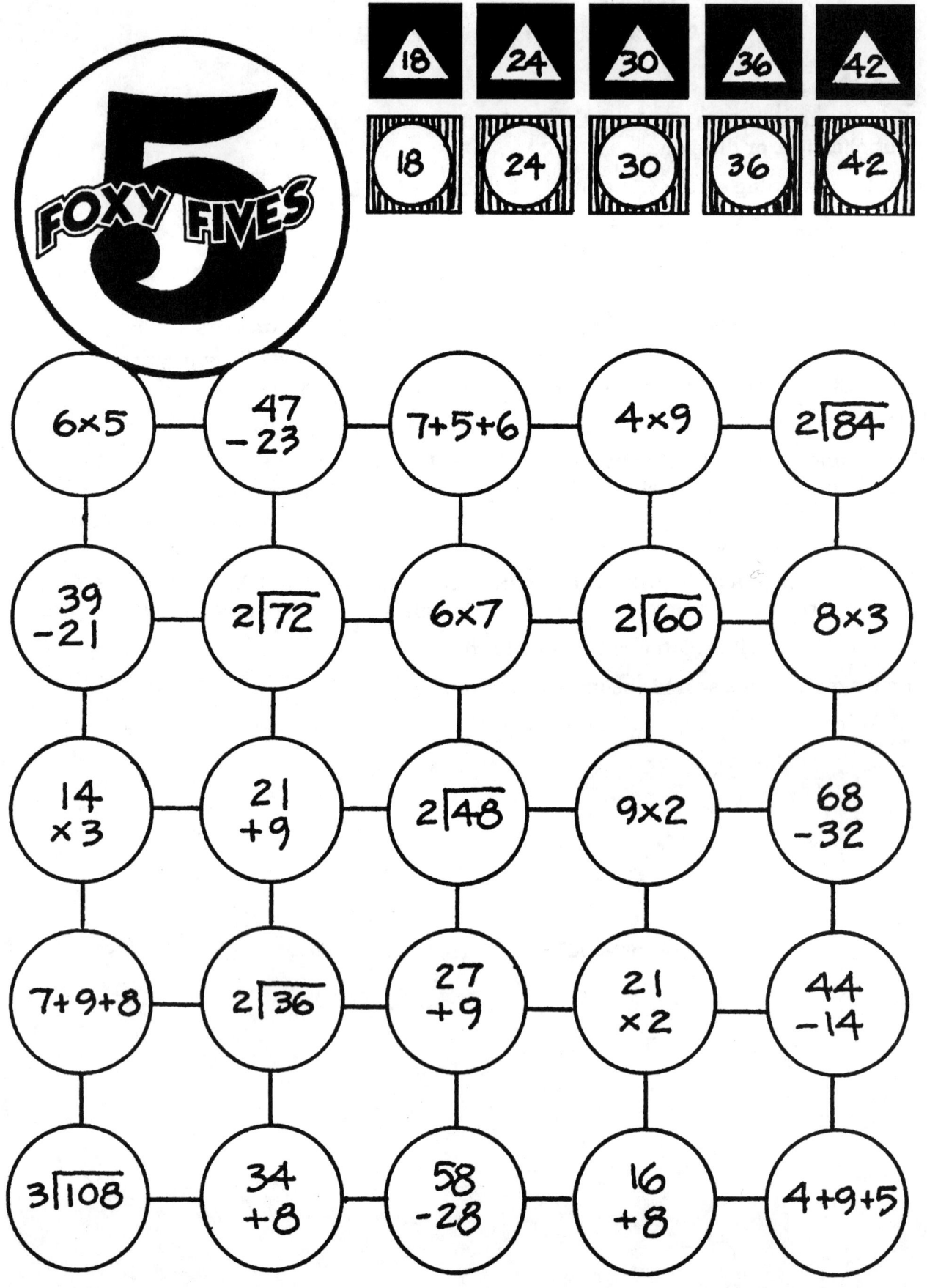

FOXY FIVES

18	24	30	36	42
18	24	30	36	42

6×5 — 47−23 — 7+5+6 — 4×9 — 2√84

39−21 — 2√72 — 6×7 — 2√60 — 8×3

14×3 — 21+9 — 2√48 — 9×2 — 68−32

7+9+8 — 2√36 — 27+9 — 21×2 — 44−14

3√108 — 34+8 — 58−28 — 16+8 — 4+9+5

Foxy Fives

Objectives

✱ Match predetermined numbers to an operation-and-algorithm (method) lattice (grid).

✱ Supply solutions to equivalent expressions.

Directions

❶ Two players share the same gameboard. Player A cuts out the squares with the five triangles and writes his or her initials on the blank side, while Player B cuts out the squares with the five circles and puts his or her initials on the blank side.

❷ The players take turns placing their markers, one at a time, on the gameboard problems. Each marker should be placed on a problem that it does *not* answer. For example, neither answer marker, ▲30 or ⓪30, can be placed on any problem whose answer is 30. It must be placed on another problem. The players check each other to make sure their markers do *not* answer the problem.

❸ Once all the markers are on the gameboard, each player takes turns sliding one of his or her markers along a line to an adjoining, unoccupied circle, with no jumping allowed. The players try to move their markers to circles whose problems those markers answer. If the marker answers the problem, the player turns over the marker on that circle. This circle and marker are now out of play.

❹ Players must move to adjoining, unoccupied circles. If a player cannot move a playable marker because all adjoining circles are occupied, he or she loses a turn. If Player A cannot move, Player B continues moving until Player A is able to move a playable marker.

❺ The winner is the player who turns over all five markers first.

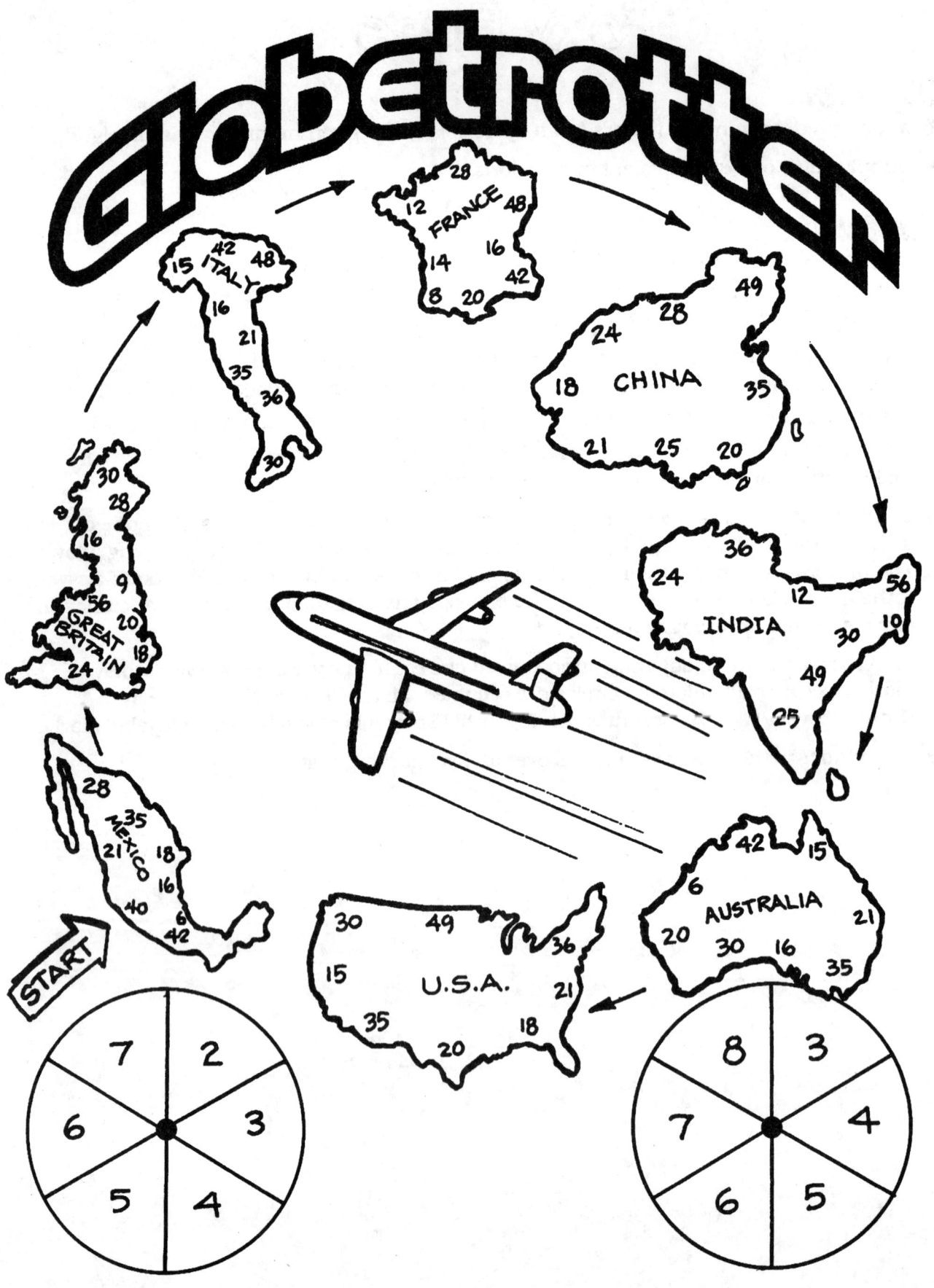

Globetrotter

Objective

✴ Recognize common multiples (products) of single-digit numbers.

Directions

❶ Two players share the "Globetrotter" gameboard. Each player has a different marker, such as a bean or a chip.

❷ The players take turns using the two spinners (see "Creating a Spinner" at the end of the instructions).

❸ Player A spins both spinners, multiplies the two numbers he or she spins, and calls out their product (multiplication answer). If a spinner lands on a line, the player uses the higher number. If the product is found in the first country, Mexico, Player A places his or her marker in that country. If this product is not in Mexico, or if a player calls out the incorrect product, the player cannot move his or her marker. Player B then takes a turn.

❹ A player may move into the next country only if the product of the two numbers is in that country; otherwise, the player does not move and his or her opponent takes a turn.

❺ Players move to the next country, following the arrows. A player cannot skip a country.

❻ The first player who reaches the last country, the United States, wins the game.

Creating a Spinner

You'll need a paper clip and a pencil.

❶ Place one end of the paper clip over the dot on the number wheel.

❷ Place the pencil point inside the paper clip on the dot.

❸ Hold the pencil firmly in place and flick the paper clip with your finger so it spins around the pencil.

❹ When the paper clip stops spinning, its tip will indicate your number.

2 sheets

BULL'S EYE

| 2 | 3 | 4 | 5 |

| 6 | 7 | 8 | 9 | 10 | 11 |

| 12 | 13 | 14 | 15 | 16 | 17 |

| 18 | 19 | 20 | 2 | 3 | 4 |

| 5 | 6 | 7 | 8 | 9 | 10 |

Bull's Eye

Objective

✳ Learn to estimate answers in multioperational sentences involving equalities and inequalities.

Directions

❶ Each player receives a "Bull's Eye" gameboard and cuts out the 28 number cards.

❷ Player A shuffles the 56 cards (2 × 28), deals three to each player, and places the remaining cards facedown in a central pile.

❸ Player B turns over a card from the central pile. This card is the target number for the cards in each player's hand.

❹ The players compete to see who can capture the target card by creating an equation with two or three cards. While creating this equation, the players keep their cards concealed from one another. When both players are finished creating the equation, they reveal their hands simultaneously. The player whose solution is closer captures the target card. For example, if the target number is 10 and Player A chooses to use all three of his or her cards to create the equation $\boxed{8} + \boxed{7} - \boxed{4} = 11$, and Player B uses two of his or her cards to create the equation $\boxed{18} \div \boxed{3} = 6$, Player A captures the target card because his or her solution is closer to 10.

❺ The player who captures the target card places the target card and the cards used in the equation to one side out of play as part of his or her score. The player who doesn't capture the target card places the cards he or she used at the bottom of the central pile and draws an equivalent number of cards from the top of the pile to bring his or her hand to three cards. The player who won the target card then draws enough cards from the top of the pile to bring his or her hand to three cards again.

❻ The players can use any combination of the four operations in their equations: addition, subtraction, multiplication, and division.

❼ In the case of a tie, neither player captures the target card. It is placed on the bottom of the deck, and a new target card is drawn. If a player makes an error, the other player captures the target card.

❽ Play continues until the entire deck is used.

❾ The player putting aside the most cards wins.

PUZZLESOME?

18 3×8 4×8 48	4×9 4×5 2×8 33	6×8 2×11 6×2 28	30 90 0 6×3	4×3 7×0 22 9×9
3×11 36 4×3 7×3	27 9×8 24 6×8	24 40 9×5 7×3	49 7×12 10×10 7×6	54 36 72 6×4
9×2 4×9 7×5 36	49 12 81 32	48 45 64 48	4×7 8 3×3 6×5	56 25 6×5 8×4
4×12 9 84 18	63 8×8 12 8×7	8×6 70 5×5 16	21 9×9 10×7 4×4	20 16 5×8 7×7
6×4 32 10×9 7×7	42 35 6×6 5×4	18 100 8×10 9×6	30 8×3 24 7×9	81 0 8×1 9×3

Puzzle Some

Numbers crossword

Adapt Yr 2 | 3 | 4 | 5

Objectives

✸ Solve a multiplication problem for one-digit numbers.

✸ Introduce the concept of exponents.

Directions

❶ Each player has a copy of the "Puzzle Some" gameboard.

❷ The players cut out the 25 cards on the gameboard.

❸ Player A shuffles all 50 cards, deals three to each player, and places the remaining cards in a central pile.

❹ Player A tries to fit his or her cards together so that all sides that touch are equal. He or she must match a problem with its answer. For example, the side with 72 must touch the side with 9 × 8, as shown:

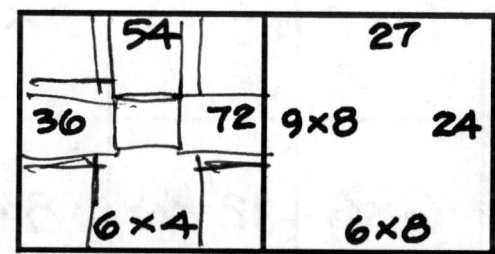

❺ In turn, each player picks a card from the central pile and tries to match it with one of his or her other cards. The player's unmatched cards can be played at a later turn. A player can match a card to an existing group or start a new group by matching two or more cards.

❻ Play continues until all the cards are used.

❼ Scoring is done by squaring the number of cards in each separate group and adding these squared numbers. For example, if a player has a group of 3 cards, a group of 5 cards, and another group of 2 cards, the group of 3 cards squared is 9 (3 × 3 = 9), the group of 5 cards squared is 25 (5 × 5 = 25), and the group of 2 cards squared is 4 (2 × 2 = 4). The player then adds 9, 25, and 4 for a score of 38.

❽ The player with the highest score wins.

SPIN OFF

2×8	3×8	4×9	6×8

6×4	4×9	8×6	3×4	2×8	7×8
4×14	2×6	8×7	8×3	3×12	4×6
2×8	3×8	6×6	12×4	8×7	12×1
28×2	12×4	4×3	4×4	6×4	8×6

8×2	8×7	3×4	6×6

12	16
56	24
48	36

Spin Off

Objective

✳ Multiply one- and two-digit numbers, with and without regrouping.

Directions

❶ The players share the same "Spin Off" gameboard. One player places a marker on the lion and the other player places a marker on the elephant at the top of the gameboard.

❷ Each player takes a turn using the spinner (see "Creating a Spinner" at the end of the instructions). The first player spins a number, and if its matching problem is in an adjoining box, he or she places the marker on that problem. If the spinner lands on a line, the player uses the higher number. For example, if the marker is on the lion, and the player spins a 36, he or she moves to the adjoining box with the problem 4 × 9. However, if the player spins a 12 and is unable to find a matching problem in an adjoining box, he or she cannot skip over boxes to find a matching problem; the player must pass and spin again on his or her next turn.

❸ Each player may progress along any path of adjoining boxes as long as he or she connects boxes from the animal at the top to the matching animal at the bottom of the gameboard.

❹ The winner is the player who first lands his or her marker on one of the three squares touching the matching animal at the bottom of the gameboard.

Creating a Spinner

You'll need a paper clip and a pencil.

❶ Place one end of the paper clip over the dot at the center of the number wheel.

❷ Place the pencil point inside the paper clip on the dot.

❸ Hold the pencil firmly in place and flick the paper clip with your finger so it spins around the pencil.

❹ When the paper clip stops spinning, its tip will indicate your number.

36

1 math game per issue

Adaptable! addition.

Grand Slam

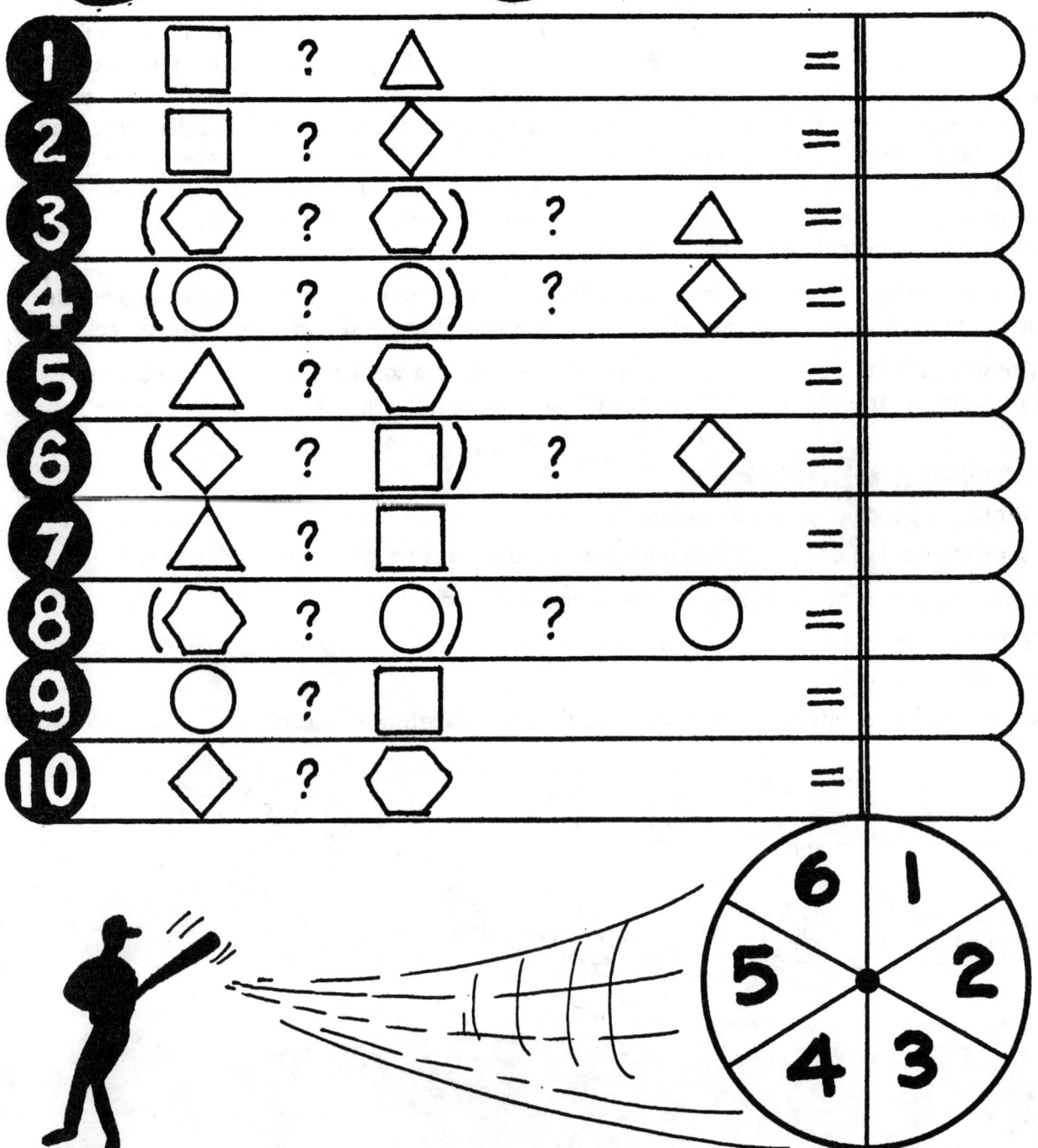

Grand Slam

Objectives

✳ Write number sentences using the distributive property of multiplication over addition (the product of the whole is equal to the sum of the products of the parts).

✳ Provide practice in solving algebraic equalities.

Directions

❶ Both players have a copy of the "Grand Slam" gameboard.

❷ The players take turns spinning a number (see "Creating a Spinner" at the end of the instructions). The player spinning decides in which shape (square, triangle, hexagon, diamond, or circle) he or she wants to place the number. For example, if Player A spins a 3 and chooses the square shape, he or she then writes 3 in all five squares on his or her own gameboard. Player B then places the 3 in any shape other than the square. Player B might decide to use 3 in the four triangles on his or her gameboard. It is now Player B's turn to spin. If Player B spins a 5, he or she writes 5 in all instances of the chosen shape. If he or she chooses a circle, 5 must be written in all the circles. Player A now has to use that 5 in a shape other than a circle on his or her gameboard. If the spinner stops on a line, the player uses the higher number.

❸ After all the shapes are filled, the players write an addition or multiplication sign over each question mark. They may use a maximum of five multiplication signs.

❹ Each player then solves the equations on his or her gameboard.

❺ After the equations are solved, each player adds the 10 answers on his or her gameboard.

❻ The player with the highest total score wins.

Creating a Spinner

You'll need a paper clip and a pencil.

❶ Place one end of the paper clip over the dot at the center of the number wheel.

❷ Place the pencil point inside the paper clip on the dot.

❸ Hold the pencil firmly in place and flick the paper clip with your finger so it spins around the pencil.

❹ When the paper clip stops spinning, its tip will indicate your number.

*Provide each
5 sets of numbers*

Kangaroo

Kangaroo

Objectives

✽ Multiply a single-digit number by a single-digit number.

✽ Apply the associative (regrouping) property of multiplication.

Directions

❶ Two players share the same gameboard.

❷ One player cuts out the 12 numbered squares, while the other cuts out the 12 numbered circles. Each player arranges his or her 12 cutouts in the first three rows on the white squares on his or her side of the board (as in checkers). The cutouts may be arranged in any order.

❸ The players follow the same rules as for checkers. When a player is about to jump an opponent's marker (cutout), he or she has to multiply the number on his or her marker by the number on the opponent's marker and call out the equation and the answer before moving. For example, if a player plans to use 8 to jump his or her opponent's 9, that player has to call out the equation 8 × 9 = 72 before moving. If a player wants to make two jumps, he or she must call the equation for each jump before moving. If a player fails to complete any equation correctly, he or she loses that move and the marker remains where it was.

❹ The winner is the player who captures all of his or her opponent's markers. If neither player can capture all of his or her opponent's markers, the game is a draw.

Yr 4 multiplic

Yr 3 addit

TRIANGLE ROUNDUP

Triangle Roundup

Objectives

✳ Practice basic facts in multiplication.

✳ Discover a winning strategy involving position.

Directions

❶ Two players share the same gameboard.

❷ The players take turns connecting any two neighboring circled numbers anywhere on the gameboard. The circled numbers are the corners of equilateral triangles.

❸ Player A first chooses two adjoining circled numbers. If Player A is able to give the correct product (multiplication answer) for these two circled numbers, he or she then connects them with a diagonal or horizontal line. Player B now chooses any two neighboring circled numbers. If Player B is unable to give the correct product, he or she cannot connect the circles and loses a turn.

❹ Connecting circled numbers continues until one player completes a triangle. The player completing the triangle places his or her initials inside it and receives one point.

❺ Play ends when all 49 possible triangles are completed.

❻ The player who has scored the most points (completed the most triangles) wins.

Yr 2 Addition
Yr 3 multip-

ROCK AROUND THE CLOCK

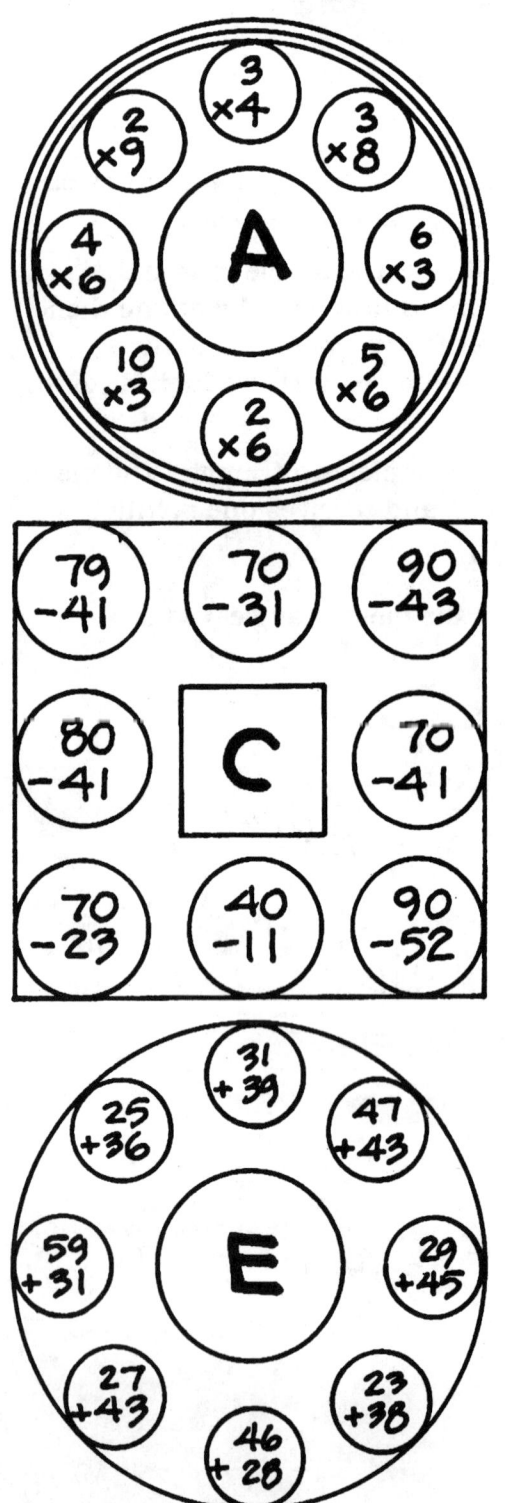

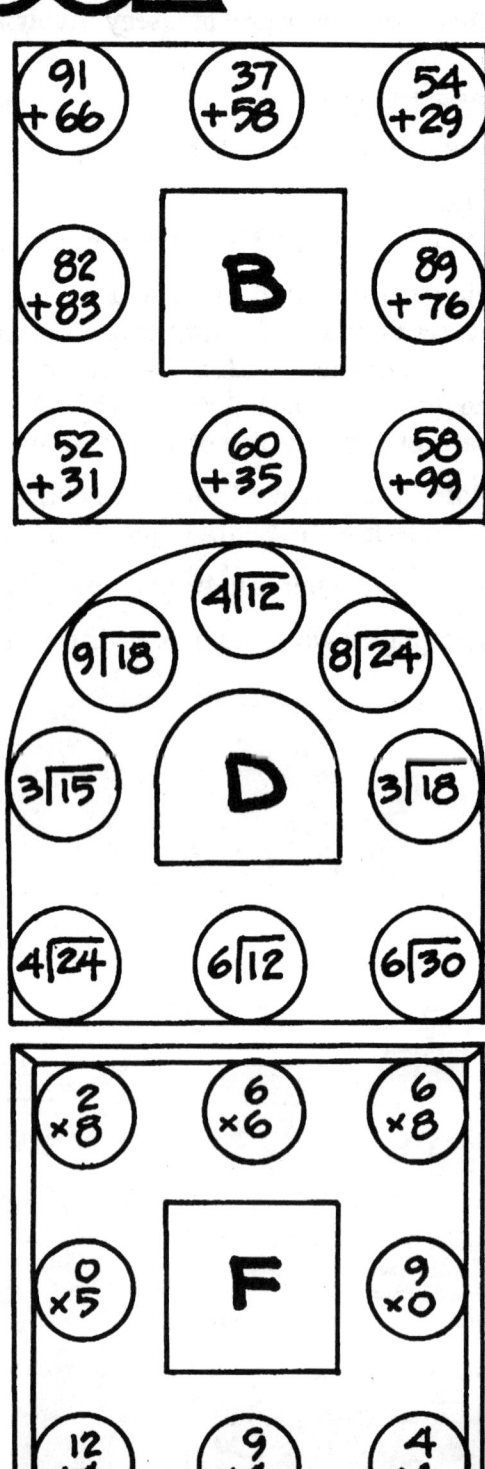

Rock Around the Clock

Objective

✹ Pair two equivalent expressions for a given number.

Directions

❶ Each player has a marker (a chip or some other type of playing piece) and a copy of the "Rock Around the Clock" gameboard. Every clock contains two problems having the same answer.

❷ The first player chooses a problem on any one of the clocks without the other player seeing his or her gameboard. For example, the first player may choose Clock E, solve the problem 47 + 43, place his marker on it, and call out "90 on Clock E."

❸ The second player finds Clock E on his or her gameboard, solves one of the problems that has an answer 90, and places his marker either on 47 + 43 or 59 + 31 (both equal 90).

❹ The two players then compare where they placed their markers. If the markers were placed on the same problems in Clock E, the second player wins the point; however, if the markers are on different problems, the first player scores the point.

❺ If the first player puts a marker on a problem but calls out an incorrect answer, the second player scores a point if he or she solves the problem correctly.

❻ The players take turns choosing a problem.

❼ The first player to score 15 points is the winner.

Trail Blazers

35−5 ●—— 3×10	40−10 —— 50−4	16+16 —— 15+15	32−12 —— 17+13	4×8 —— 13+33	24+8 —— 25−5
10×2 ——● 20+0	20+10 ——● 40−10	17+29 —— 30+2	16+30 ——● 54−8	12+20 —— 14+6	18+14 —— 4×5
62−30 —— 10+10	15+17 —— 13+7	50−18 —— 12+8	44−8 —— 40−20	26+6 —— 33−13	5×6 —— 15+21
20+26 —— 17+13	15×2 —— 19+27	50−4 —— 50−20	22+8 —— 39+7	24+6 —— 54−8	18+28 —— 18+12

Trail Blazers

Objective

✳ Perform a binary operation (add, subtract, multiply, or divide) in matching two equivalent expressions.

Directions

❶ Two players share the same "Trail Blazer" gameboard and cut out the 24 cards resembling dominoes. Each of 20 domino cards has two problems with different answers. The remaining four cards have problems with the same answers. These four cards have dots.

❷ Player A places one of the cards with a dot faceup on the table. He or she shuffles the remaining cards, deals four to each player, and puts the rest facedown in a central pile. Neither player sees the other's cards.

❸ Player B begins by matching half of one of his or her cards to the card that is faceup. For example, if [35−5 ● 3×10] is faceup,

Player B can match the half [40-10] by joining its side, at the dot, to the card on the

table as follows:

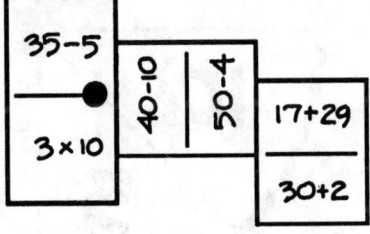

Player A now matches half of one of his or her cards, for example [17+29] ,

to the [50-4] on the table by joining the cards side to side as follows:

The cards may branch out in any direction.

❹ If a player cannot match a card on the table, he or she draws a card from the central pile and passes.

❺ If a player makes a mismatch, he or she takes the card back and loses a turn.

❻ Play continues until all the cards in the central pile are used.

❼ The player who has the least number of cards left in his or her hand is the winner.

Rotten Apple

Objective

✳ Extend sums involving unseen addends and regrouping in multidigit addition.

Directions

❶ Two players share the same "Rotten Apple" gameboard.

❷ The game can start on any wheel. Both players take turns spinning on the same wheel (see "Creating a Spinner" at the end of the instructions). Each player spins as many times in a row as he or she wishes, writes down each number, and keeps a total score. If the spinner stops on a line, the player takes the higher number.

❸ A player spins on a wheel until he or she decides to stop or spins a rotten apple. If a player continues spinning and lands on a rotten apple, his or her total for that wheel is wiped out.

❹ If Player A decides to take four turns on a wheel and spins 3, 7, 5, and 9, he or she adds these numbers for a score of 24. Player B then takes his or her turns on the same wheel. If Player B decides to take five turns on that wheel and spins 9, 5, 8, 9, and a rotten apple, his or her score for the four previous spins is wiped out, and the score for that wheel is 0.

❺ The players alternate going first on each wheel.

❻ The player who has the highest total score for all the wheels wins the game.

Creating a Spinner

You'll need a paper clip and a pencil.

❶ Place one end of the paper clip over the dot on the number wheel.

❷ Place the pencil point inside the paper clip on the dot.

❸ Hold the pencil firmly in place and flick the paper clip with your finger so it spins around the pencil.

❹ When the paper clip stops spinning, its tip will indicate your number.

Yr 3 adding + multiply

pícasso

12	30	9	17	31	16	7	8	11	5	31	4
7	3	6	21	23	32	25	3	13	18	11	26
2	19	11	28	8	14	7	18	12	8	23	6
13	20	33	25	28	17	9	29	18	24	6	19
26	16	4	18	10	30	28	6	5	11	18	10
1	5	27	31	9	29	33	10	29	22	32	30
12	32	18	4	6	10	19	5	24	31	11	21
26	8	29	30	1	33	7	19	28	23	18	32
16	14	26	11	29	8	18	10	29	4	15	11
33	19	4	17	8	33	9	21	16	11	32	26
18	9	26	30	33	16	13	31	18	9	5	28
27	30	20	6	10	19	32	17	30	27	33	10

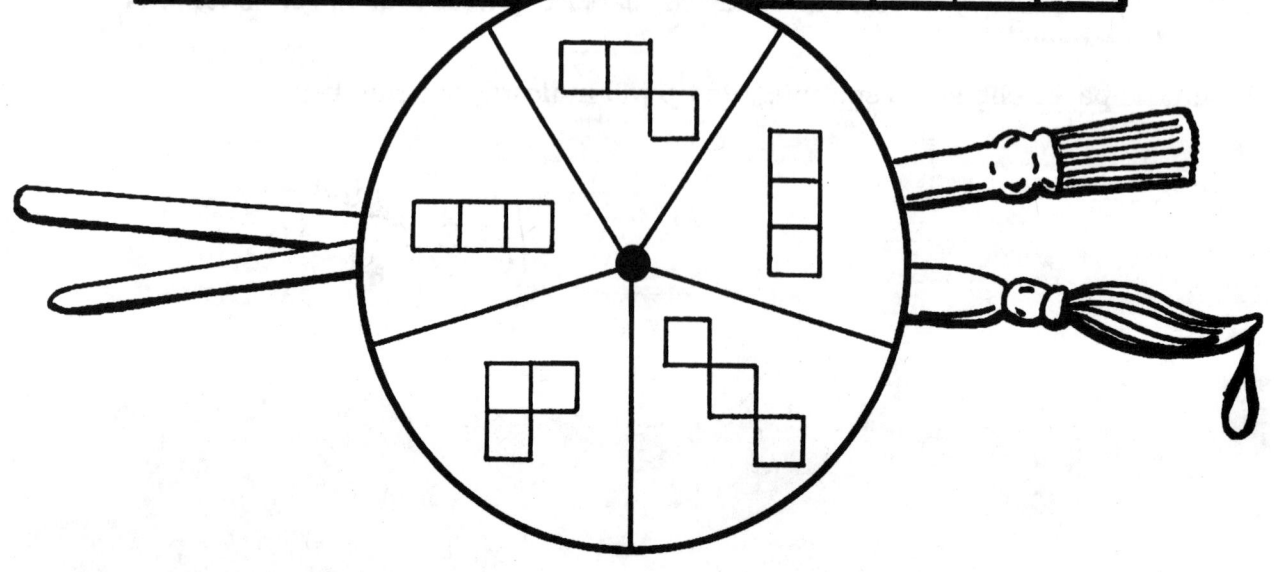

Picasso

Objectives

✳ Determine the sum for a set of three numbers, with and without regrouping.

✳ Visualize how different combinations of three squares fit onto a 12-by-12 grid.

Directions

❶ Two players share the same "Picasso" gameboard.

❷ One player uses a red crayon; the other uses a blue crayon.

❸ Player A starts the game. He or she places a small dot in the upper, right-hand corner of a number box in the top row. Player A then spins a pattern (see "Creating a Spinner" at the end of the instructions). If the spinner stops on a line, the player may choose either pattern. Using the dotted box as one of the squares in the pattern, the player adds the three numbers in that pattern and calls out their sum. For example, if Player A marked a dot in | 31 | and spins the pattern | | | | , he or she may add the three number boxes | 17 || 31 || 16 | , or any other three boxes of the same pattern that include dotted Box 31. Player A might have chosen | 9 || 17 || 31 | or | 31 || 16 || 7 | . The player adds 17 + 31 + 16 and calls out their sum, 64. On scratch paper, each player keeps track of his or her own totals.

❹ If Player A calls out the correct sum, he or she then colors the three boxes. Once a box has been colored, it cannot be reused.

❺ A player loses a turn if he or she calls out an incorrect sum or if the pattern cannot be used because the needed number boxes already have been colored.

❻ Player B now selects a number box from a row close to the top of the gameboard and spins a pattern.

❼ Play ends when both players are unable to color a pattern for three turns.

❽ The player with the highest total score wins.

Creating a Spinner

You'll need a paper clip and a pencil.

❶ Place one end of the paper clip over the dot on the number wheel.

❷ Place the pencil point inside the paper clip on the dot.

❸ Hold the pencil firmly in place and flick the paper clip with your finger so it spins around the pencil.

❹ When the paper clip stops spinning, its tip will indicate your number.

EQUATOR-GATOR

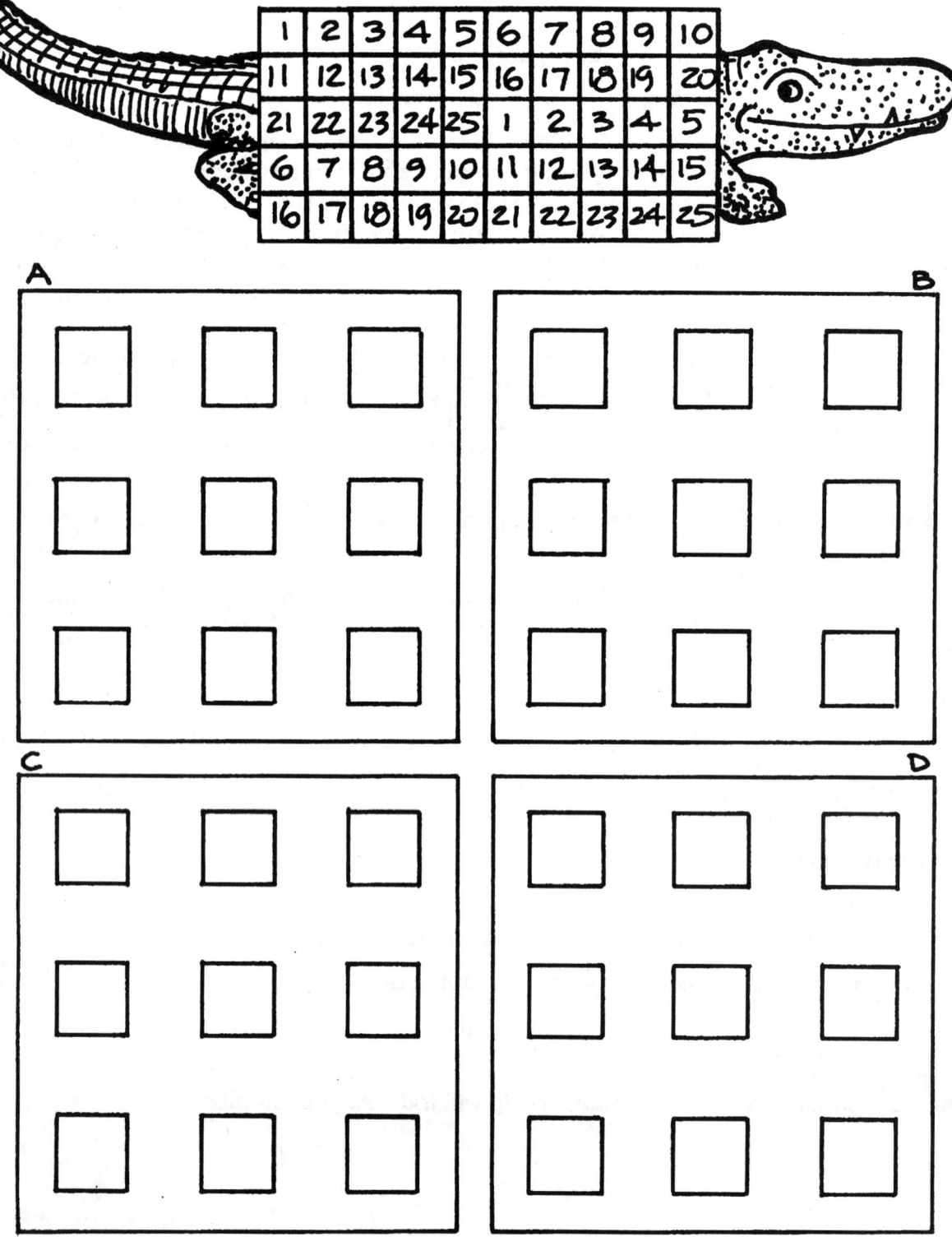

1	2	3	4	5	6	7	8	9	10
11	12	13	14	15	16	17	18	19	20
21	22	23	24	25	1	2	3	4	5
6	7	8	9	10	11	12	13	14	15
16	17	18	19	20	21	22	23	24	25

A

B

C

D

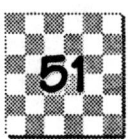

Equator-Gator

Objective

✸ Create equations in three-by-three matrices (grids).

Directions

❶ Two players share the same "Equator-Gator" gameboard.

❷ One player crosses out a number from the grid at the top of the gameboard and writes it in an empty box in Set A. Then the other player crosses out a different number and places it in another box in Set A.

❸ The players alternate filling boxes in Set A until a horizontal, vertical, or diagonal line of three boxes can be formed.

❹ The player who fills in the last empty box in a horizontal, vertical, or diagonal line tries to complete an equation with these three boxes regardless of who filled in the other two boxes. He or she completes the equation by supplying the necessary signs between the boxes. The player may supply an addition, a subtraction, a multiplication, or a division sign, and an equal sign.

❺ Each player keeps a record of his or her equations by drawing a circle or a triangle around the box containing the answer he or she supplied.

❻ Once a number has been crossed out, it may not be used again. If a number does not appear in the grid, it may not be used to solve equations.

❼ After all the boxes of Set A have been filled in, the players move on to Set B. The players take turns starting each set. If the players cannot fill in a box because the numbers that would complete the equation have already been used or do not appear on the grid, they may leave the box empty.

❽ A player scores one point for each equation he or she completes.

❾ The player who scores the most points after all sets of boxes have been used is the winner.

CIRCLE-A-GO-GO

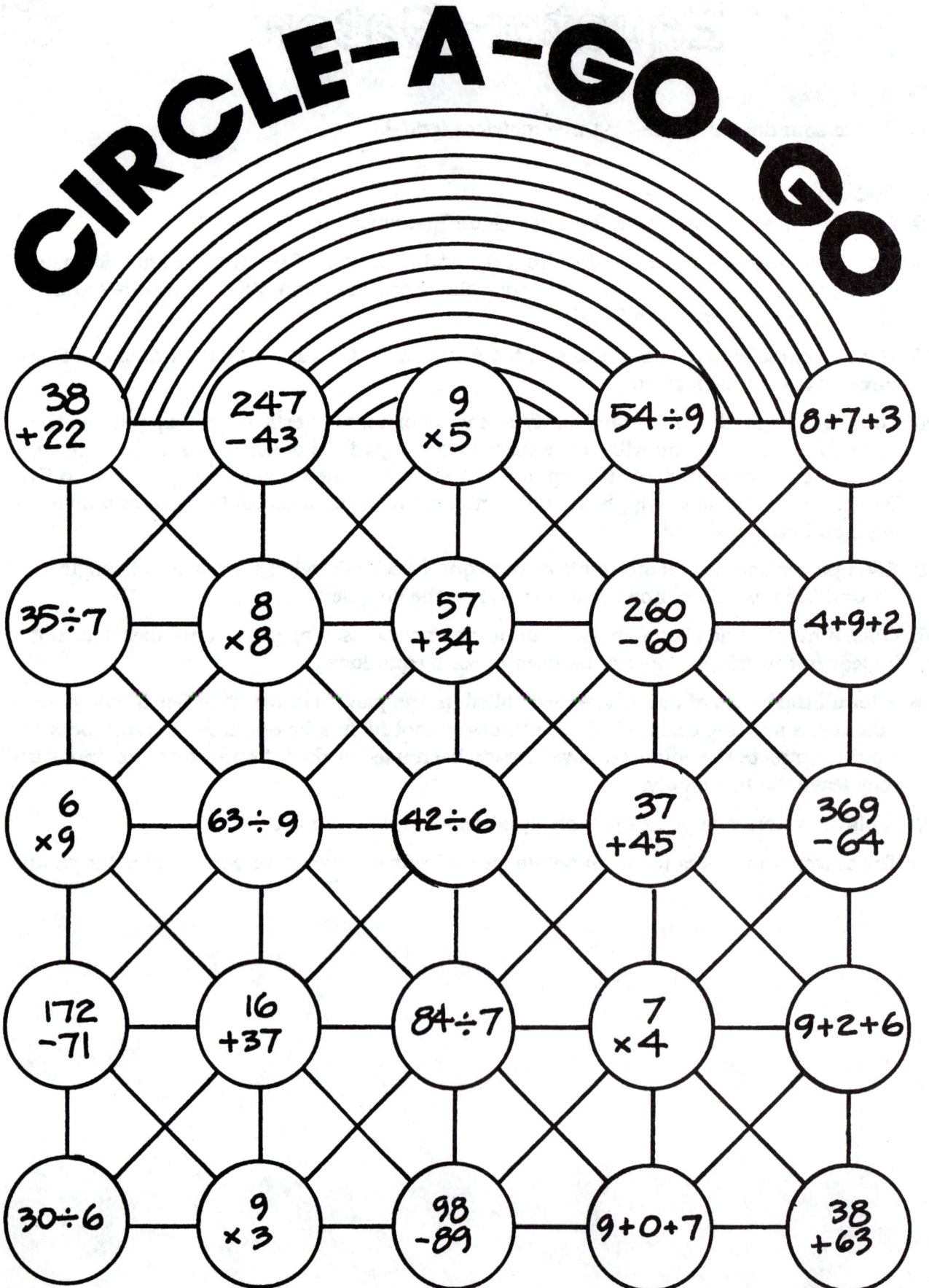

Circle-A-Go-Go

Objectives

❋ Solve multioperational expressions.

❋ Discover winning strategies.

Directions

❶ Two players share the same "Circle-A-Go-Go" gameboard.

❷ Each player has four markers or chips.

❸ Each player takes a turn solving a problem and calling out its answer. The player then places one of his or her markers on that circle.

❹ This procedure continues until each player has all four markers on the gameboard.

❺ The players take turns sliding one of their markers along a line to an adjoining circle as they call out the answer to the problem in that circle.

❻ If a player solves a problem incorrectly, he or she may not move a marker.

❼ A player can move only to a circle that has no marker. No jumping is allowed.

❽ Sliding continues until one player is able to position his or her four markers in a diagonal, horizontal, or vertical line, or a small square made of adjacent circles. That player wins.

❾ Examples of winning positions:

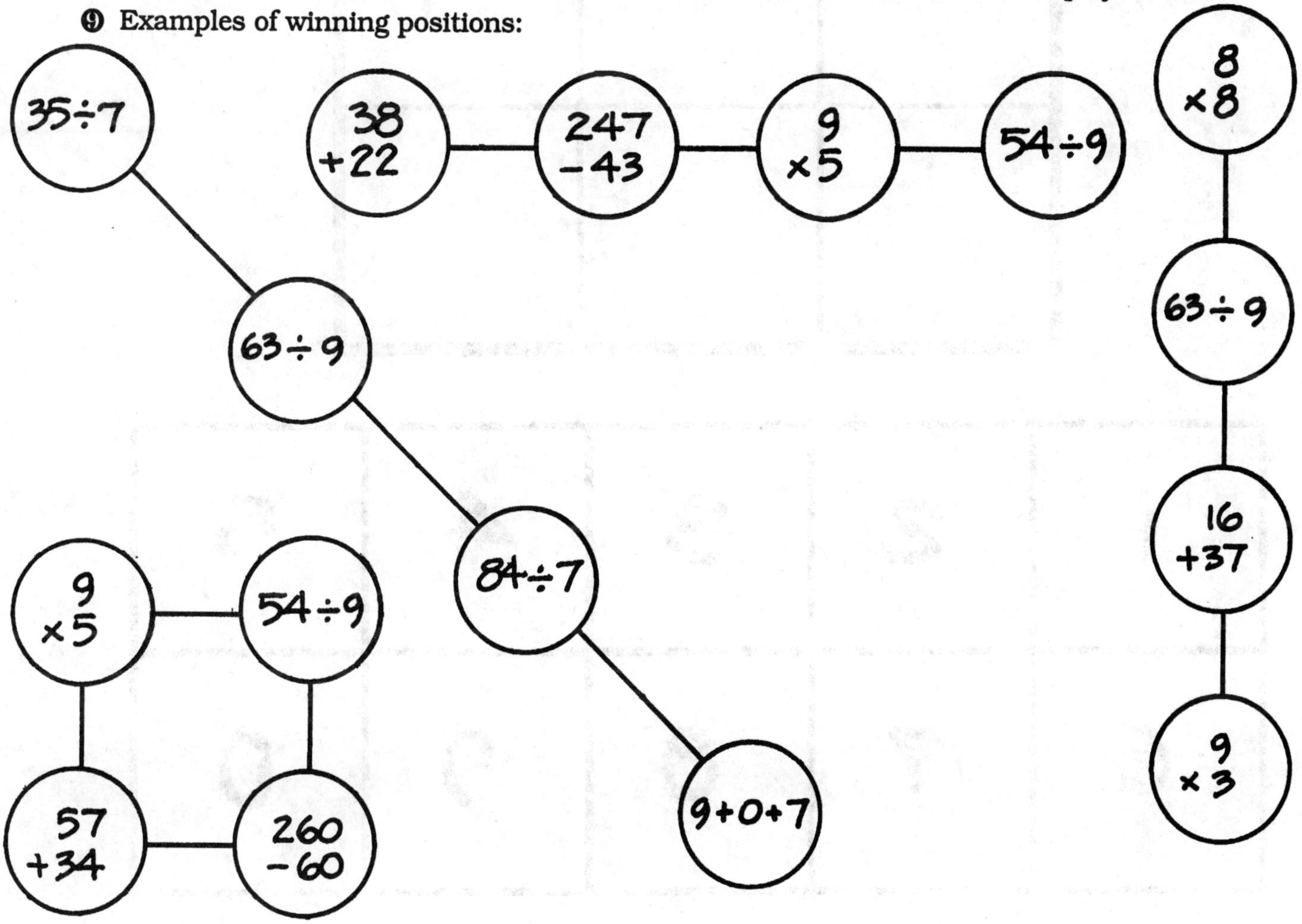

LINE UP

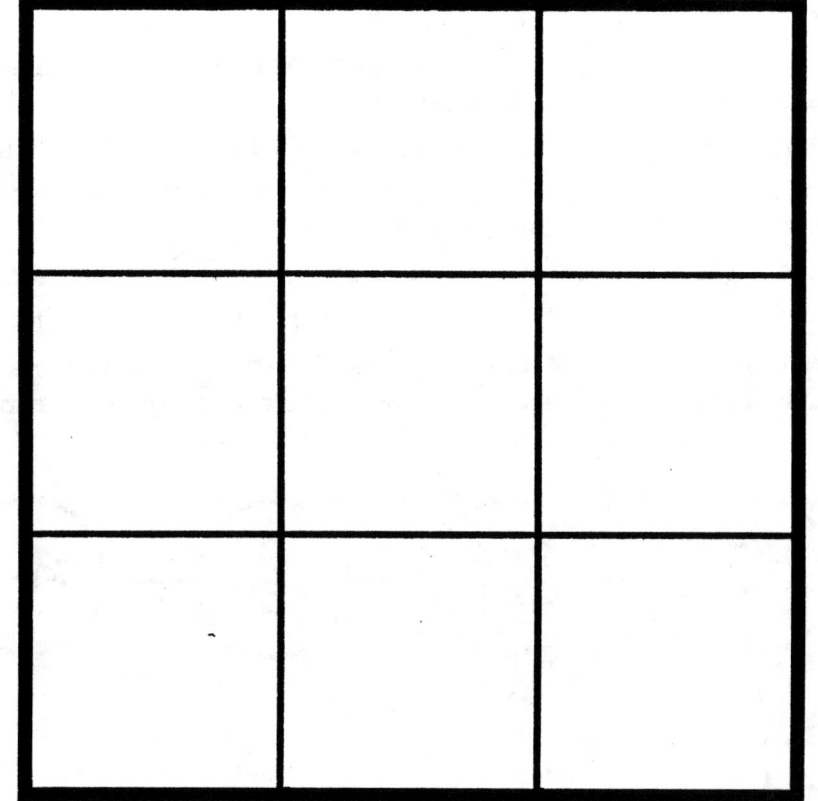

1	2	3	4	5
6	7	8	9	0

Line Up

Objectives

✳ Complete a number sentence using a missing addend.

✳ Learn about constructing magic squares.

Directions

❶ The players share the same "Line Up" gameboard.

❷ One player cuts out the cards numbered 0 through 9 and places them face up on the table.

❸ Each player alternates picking a card and placing it anywhere on the grid. For example, one player picks 8 and places it in the uppermost right-hand corner, while the other picks 7 and places it immediately below his opponent's card.

❹ The players continue placing cards on the grid until three cards in a line add up to equal 15. The line can be diagonal, horizontal, or vertical, and there must be three cards in the line.

❺ The player who first completes a line wins the game.

❻ If neither player makes 15, the game is a tie.

Variation

Instead of picking any card from the set, one player uses the even numbers and the other uses odd numbers. The game continues as usual following steps 3 through 6 in the directions.

SWITCHBOARD

8	5	10	2	11	4	7	6	5
1	8	11	3	6	7	9	2	7
9	6	7	1	8	3	5	10	3
12	2	10	12	4	8	5	4	9
7	13	15	5	15	9	2	6	14
10	3	12	4	9	1	14	9	2
4	6	15	2	10	8	6	4	13
3	14	1	12	4	13	3	15	12
14	11	8	5	10	2	6	12	5

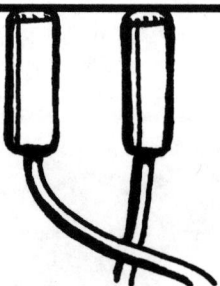

TARGET ◯ NUMBER

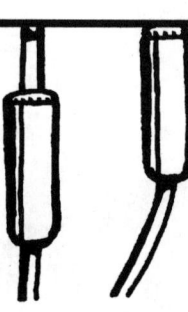

Switchboard

Objective

✹ Construct number sentences for one- and two-digit numbers involving the operation of addition, subtraction, multiplication, or division.

Directions

❶ Each player has a "Switchboard" gameboard.

❷ The teacher gives the class a target number from 6 to 12. For example, the teacher chooses 9 as the target number. Each pupil then writes 9 in the target number circle at the bottom of the gameboard.

❸ Each player connects two numbers anywhere on the gameboard that equal the target number 9. Players may use addition, subtraction, multiplication, or division in their equations. The players must connect the numbers by circling each number and drawing a line between the two circles. The line cannot go through a number. A player may not reuse a circled number.

❹ The teacher gives the class 15 minutes to make as many equations as possible.

❺ After 15 minutes, the players exchange gameboards and check each other's equations. The winner is the player with the most equations.

SUPER TIC-TAC-TOE

600 −348	769 +768	800 −573	876 +773	900 −643
367 +265	700 −488	379 +266	500 −278	259 +256
600 −338	968 +958	901 −239	999 +999	905 −288
968 +958	404 −262	499 +469	609 −472	589 +487
820 −289	696 +344	720 −191	566 +534	404 −262

Super Tic-Tac-Toe

Objectives

✳ Practice multidigit addition and subtraction with regrouping.

✳ Devise strategies for aligning markers on a five-by-five grid.

Directions

❶ Two players share the same "Super Tic-Tac-Toe" gameboard. Each player has 13 markers (chips, for example) of a different color than his or her opponent's.

❷ Each player takes a turn solving a problem on scratch paper before he or she places a marker on that square on the gameboard.

❸ The players try to make as many tic-tac-toes as possible by aligning their markers in a line either horizontally, vertically, or diagonally. The players also try to block each other from making a tic-tac-toe.

❹ A marker may belong to more than one tic-tac-toe.

❺ Play continues until all squares are covered.

❻ Each player counts his or her tic-tac-toes and totals the points. Points are awarded as follows: Three in a row counts for 1 point; four in a row counts for 3 points and five in a row counts for 5 points.

❼ If a player solves a problem incorrectly, he or she loses a turn.

❽ The player with the most points wins.

GRAB IT

9	1	3	7	5	6
8	4	2	3	8	7
1	5	4	2	6	9

18	32	64	35	27
72	56	36	40	24
25	30	45	54	21
16	42	81	12	20
48	63	28	14	15

Grab It

Objective

✴ Identify two factors that equal a product (multiplication answer).

Directions

❶ Each player has a copy of the "Grab It" gameboard.

❷ Each player cuts out the set of cards numbered 1 through 9 and places them faceup on the table.

❸ One player cuts out the 25 product cards, shuffles them, and places them facedown in a central pile.

❹ A player turns over a product card from the central pile and tries to match the product card by multiplying two of his or her number cards. For example, a player turns over the product card ◈24◈ and matches it by multiplying number cards 3 and 8.

❺ Each player has to show his or her opponent the two cards he or she uses to match the product card. If the player multiplies correctly, he or she takes the product card and either one of the two number cards and puts them aside out of play. In the example above, the player would take the product card ◈24◈ and either the number card 3 or the number card 8 and place these two cards aside, out of play.

❻ If the player multiplies incorrectly, he or she returns the product card to the bottom of the pile.

❼ The players alternate turning over the product cards until none are left or until four consecutive product cards are turned over without any being taken. The game then ends.

❽ The players count the number of cards they have each taken out of play. The player who has put aside the most cards wins.

Leftovers

| 37 | 11 | 81 | 15 | 58 | 34 | 10 | GO |

| 59 | | 52 | 25 | 51 | 72 | 26 | 50 |

| 83 | 73 | | | | | | 71 |

| 13 | 29 | | 6 | 7 | | | 44 |

| 38 | 53 | | | | | | 66 |

| 60 | 75 | | 9 | 8 | | | 22 |

| 85 | 31 | 55 | 77 | 79 | 57 | | |

| 39 | | | | | 33 | | 47 |

| 61 | | | | | | | 67 |

| 17 | 41 | 62 | 19 | 43 | 65 | 20 | 23 |

Leftovers

Objective

✳ Divide a two-digit number by a one-digit number with remainders.

Directions

❶ Two players share the same "Leftovers" gameboard.

❷ Each player takes a turn spinning (see "Creating a Spinner" at the end of the instructions). The player who spins the higher number goes first. If the spinner stops on a line, the player takes the higher number.

❸ The first player places his or her marker on GO and spins a number. He or she takes that number and divides it into 10 (the first number after GO). The remainder in the answer determines how many places the player can move the marker. For example, Player A spins 7 and then divides 7 into 10 and gets 1 with a remainder of 3. Player A then moves 3 squares past 10 and places his or her marker on 15. Player B now takes a turn, spins 6, and divides it into 10, getting 1 with a remainder of 4. Player B then moves 4 squares past 10 and places his or her marker on 81.

❹ For each spin, the players divide the number they spin into the number where their markers previously landed. In the above example, for their next turns, Player A divides the number he or she spins into 15 and Player B divides into 81.

❺ If the remainder is zero, the player stays in place.

❻ If a player gives an incorrect answer, he or she loses a turn.

❼ The first player who reaches the cheese wins the game.

Creating a Spinner

You'll need a paper clip and a pencil.

❶ Place one end of the paper clip over the dot in the center of the number wheel.

❷ Place the pencil point inside the paper clip on the dot.

❸ Hold the pencil firmly in place and flick the paper clip with your finger so it spins around the pencil.

❹ When the paper clip stops spinning, its tip will indicate your number.

STACK 'EM UP

75 -45	63 +37	7 × 8	98 -58	42÷7	6 × 9	56 +44
45 +55	63÷9	81÷9	57 +43	134 +16	150 -50	6+9+5
8+9+3	200 -100	6+4+10	8×9	101 -1	17 +13	3 × 9
9 × 7	75 +25	36÷4	4+7+9	72÷9	125 -25	130 +20
30÷6	64÷8	105 -5	72÷8	4+9+2	4 × 8	36÷9
50 -45	120 +80	8×5	3+4+3	38 +22	54÷9	172 -72

Stack 'Em Up

Objectives

✳ Solve multioperational problems.

✳ Explore strategies in a six-by-seven matrix (grid).

Directions

❶ Two players share the same "Stack 'Em Up" gameboard. Each player has 21 markers (chips or beans) of a different color than his or her opponent's.

❷ Starting at the bottom of the board and moving up, the players take turns solving a problem and calling out its answer before placing a marker on that circle.

❸ The first player chooses a problem to solve on the bottom row. The second player may choose another problem anywhere on the bottom row or directly above his or her opponent's.

❹ A player may advance to another row only if a marker is directly beneath the circle he or she wants to move to in that row.

❺ Play continues until one player places four of his or her markers in neighboring circles that make a horizontal, vertical, or diagonal line. The players try to block each other from making a winning move.

❻ If a player solves the problem incorrectly, he or she cannot place a marker and loses that turn.

❼ A player can only choose a circle that has no marker on it.

❽ The player who first places four markers in a horizontal, diagonal, or vertical line wins the game.

BANKER$ DELIGHT

+	44	49	45	42	47	48
18						
13						
15						
14						
16						
17						

Banker's Delight

Objectives

✸ Perform multidigit addition in your head.

✸ Determine equivalent coordinate pairs for given sums.

Directions

❶ Two players each have a copy of the "Banker's Delight" gameboard. Each player has 10 beans or other markers.

❷ Player A takes three beans and places each one in a square where two numbers intersect on the gameboard. For example, he or she may place them in the squares where 13 and 45 intersect, where 13 and 47 intersect, and where 14 and 49 intersect. Player A adds each pair and tells Player B the sums: 58 (13 + 45), 60 (13 + 47), and 63 (14 + 49). Using these sums as clues, Player B tries to duplicate Player A's gameboard by placing beans in the same squares on his or her own gameboard. Player B may place beans in squares where 14 and 44 intersect (for the sum of 58), where 13 and 47 intersect (for the sum of 60), and where 18 and 45 intersect (for the sum of 63).

❸ A player may use only one bean per square. Neither player should see the other's gameboard while he or she is placing beans.

❹ After Player B has tried to match Player A's squares, the players compare their gameboards. If Player B has matched any of Player A's squares, Player B captures both players' beans for that square. When Player B has not matched Player A, Player A keeps both players' beans. In this example, Player B captures the beans where 13 and 47 intersect because they are on the same squares, but loses the others because they are not on the same squares as Player A's beans. Captured beans are placed in the rectangle at the top of the gameboard, which serves as the "bank."

❺ The game continues with each player taking turns going first until one of them has captured eight beans. That player is the winner.

PARTNERS

5X5	6X3	3X3	7X3	5X6
9X8	8X7	6X4	4X8	8X8
6X8	9X7	4X9	6X7	8X5
25	21	56	24	63
9	72	32	64	42
18	30	48	36	40

Partners

Objective

✳ Associate factor pairs with their products (multiplication answers).

Directions

❶ Two players share the same gameboard.

❷ One player cuts out 30 cards and places them at random facedown on the table.

❸ Player A turns over two cards. If these cards match, he or she takes the cards. For example, if Player A turns over the two cards 8×7 and 56, he or she takes these cards because they match. If the cards do not match, the player leaves them faceup. Player B now turns over two more cards and matches any cards that are *faceup* on the table.

❹ Each player alternates until all the cards are turned over.

❺ The player who accumulates the most cards wins.

❻ The players can reshuffle the cards and play more games.

SharpShooter

Spinner I: 1, 10, 20, 30, 40, 50

Spinner II: 9, 2, 8, 3, 7, 4, 6, 5

Target: 1, 2, 4, 8, 16, 32

Sharpshooter

Objectives

✱ In your head, add and subtract numbers that are powers of 2 to equal any other whole number.

✱ Explore the additive nature of the binary number system—by adding together numbers that are powers of 2, you can get all the whole numbers.

Directions

❶ Each player has a copy of the gameboard and 12 beans to be used as markers.

❷ The players take turns spinning both of the wheels (see "Creating a Spinner" at the end of the instructions). The number that Player A spins determines the target number that both players must use. To get the target number, Player A adds together the numbers he or she spun. For example, if the spinner lands on 30 on Wheel I and 7 on Wheel II, Player A adds 30 and 7 to get the target number, 37. If a spinner lands on a line, the player uses the higher number.

❸ Each player places beans or other markers on the circles on the target that add up to the target number, using the fewest possible beans. Using 37 as the example target number, a player might place a bean in the circle marked 1, a second bean in the circle marked 4, and a third bean in the circle marked 32. Using 3 beans, this player creates the sum of 37.

❹ The player who first gets the target number with the least number of beans records the target number as his or her score on scratch paper.

❺ The players reuse all their beans, and player B spins for a new target number.

❻ Play ends after each player has three turns to spin for the target number. The winner is the player with the highest total.

Creating a Spinner

You'll need a paper clip and a pencil.

❶ Place one end of the paper clip over the center of the number wheel.

❷ Place the pencil point inside the paper clip on the center of the wheel.

❸ Hold the pencil firmly in place and flick the paper clip with your finger so it spins around the pencil.

❹ When the paper clip stops spinning, its tip will indicate your number.

SHUFFLEBOARD

× 8	+ 10	× 7	− 5	× 12
− 12	− 4	+ 9	+ 15	− 10
+ 8	× 5	+ 3	× 7	− 5
− 3	× 4	− 8	+ 6	× 4
× 1	× 2	− 3	+ 2	× 3

Shuffleboard

Objective

✸ Compute a series of operations involving single-digit and double-digit numbers.

Directions

❶ The players share the same "Shuffleboard" gameboard.

❷ Each player takes turns placing a disk (a coin or chip) in the START circle and pushing it onto the shuffleboard. The player uses the first number his or her disk lands on as the starting number, ignoring its sign. If the disk lands on two or more squares, the player takes the highest number.

❸ After each turn, a player removes the disk from the shuffleboard. Players may use paper and pencil to compute the scores.

❹ For each subsequent turn, players perform the operation with the number on which the disk lands. If the disk lands on two or more squares, the player does the operation indicated by the largest number. If the disk stops at an intersection, the player does the operation indicated by the largest number. For example, if Player A's first number is 5, and the disk next lands on the ×4 , Player A multiplies 5 × 4, scoring 20 points. If Player B's first number is 6 and the disk stops at the intersection of these four squares:

−4	+9
×5	+3

Player B adds 6 + 9, scoring 15 points. After two turns, Player A's score is 20 and Player B's score is 15.

❺ If a player makes a mistake, he or she scores no points for that turn. If the disk goes off the gameboard, the player loses a turn. If a player lands on a square with a minus sign, and his or her score is lower than the number to be subtracted, his or her score becomes 0. No score can go below 0.

❻ Play continues until one player scores 500 or more points. That player wins the game.

Double Cross

Objectives
✳ Subtract one- and two-digit numbers, with and without regrouping.

✳ Relate coordinate geometry (position) to number operations.

Directions
❶ Each player receives a "Double Cross" gameboard.

❷ In random order, the players write the numbers 6 through 30 in the 25 circles on their gameboards, with every circle having a different number. Once a player places a number in a circle, she or he crosses it out on top of the gameboard. The players must not see each other's gameboards.

❸ Each player takes a turn choosing a coordinate (locating a circle) by calling the letter-number combination. The player calls the letter first and the number second.

❹ Following this procedure, the players locate the number circle for the called coordinate. If Player A calls the coordinate B-4, both players locate B-4 on their gameboards. On Player A's gameboard, B-4 might be 15, while on Player B's gameboard, B-4 might be 9.

❺ The players then subtract the smaller number from the larger to determine the points to be scored. In the above example, they perform the equation 15 – 9 = 6. Since Player A's number was larger, Player A scores the 6 points.

❻ For each turn, the players record their scores and keep running totals on scatch paper.

❼ If both circles have the same number, neither player records a score.

❽ Each player crosses out the number circle once it has been used. These coordinates cannot be chosen again.

❾ If a player subtracts incorrectly, he or she scores no points for that turn and does not cross out the number circle. Either player may reuse this coordinate at a later turn.

❿ The game continues until all the circles are used. The player with the highest score wins.

Variation
If younger players cannot add their scores easily, have them place markers (such as beans) over each number circle on their gameboards after Step 2. The player who does the subtraction correctly takes the beans off both gameboards and places them aside. In case of a tie, each player takes his or her own bean off the gameboard. When all the beans have been removed from the gameboards, the player with the most beans wins.

FILL 'ER UP

2	2	2	2	2	2
3	3	3	3	3	3
4	4	4	4	4	4
6	6	6	6	6	6

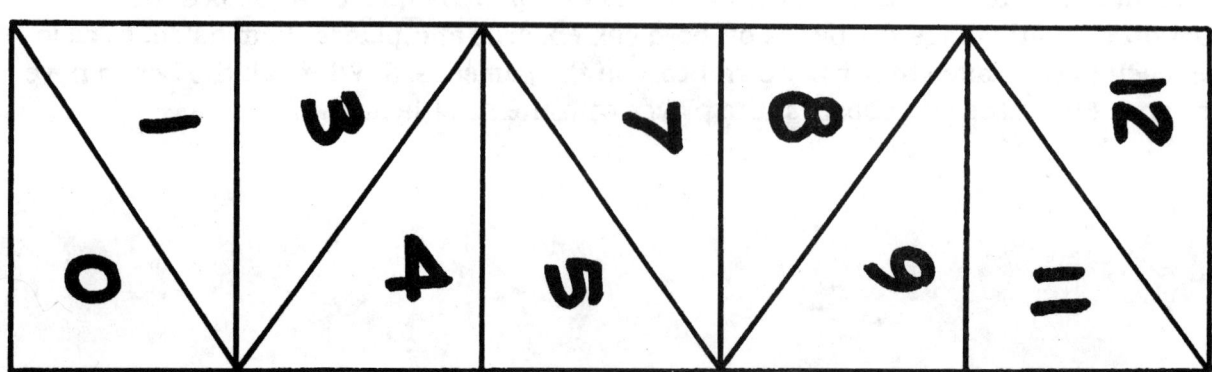

Fill 'Er Up

Objective

✳ Construct number sentences involving three operations that equal a given number.

Directions

❶ Both players have a copy of the "Fill 'Er Up" gameboard.

❷ Each player cuts out the 24 square number cards and places them face up on the table. Each number from 2 to 6 has six cards.

❸ One player cuts out the 10 triangle answer cards, shuffles them, and places them face down in a central pile.

❹ Each player alternates turning over an answer card from the central pile. Both players try to complete an equation for this answer card. They may use addition, subtraction, or both. If the answer card 11 is turned over, one player's equation might be $6 + 2 + 3$, while the other player's equation might be $6 + 4 + 3 - 2$.

❺ Once a player uses the number cards in an equation they are placed aside, out of play.

❻ The players score a point for every equation they can make.

❼ The game continues until all 10 answer cards are turned over.

❽ The player with the most points wins the game.

PUT ON

A

1	2	3
4	5	6
7	8	9

B

4	5	6
8	9	10
1	2	3

C

1	3	5
2	4	6
7	8	10

Put On

Objective

✳ Add two or more single-digit numbers, recognizing that a sum can be partitioned into many subgroups.

Directions

❶ Each player receives a copy of the "Put On" gameboard.

❷ Play begins on Grid A. One player spins (see "Creating a Spinner" at the end of the instructions). If the spinner lands on a line, the player takes the higher number. The player places a bean or beans on the number spun or any combination that adds up to that sum. For example, if the player spun a 9, he or she has a choice of covering 9 or any combination that would add up to 9: 5 and 4; 6 and 3; 4, 3, and 2, etc.

❸ The other player now spins. If the player spins a 3, he or she has only two ways of putting beans on Grid A: 2 and 1 or 3.

❹ Play stops on Grid A when either a player is unable to put a bean on it after two spins or all the numbers on each player's grid are covered—whichever occurs first. The players do not have to stop at the same time.

❺ Once play has stopped on Grid A, the players add the numbers covered by their beans. These totals are their scores for Grid A.

❻ Players alternate being first to spin.

❼ The game continues until Grids A, B, and C have been used.

❽ The player with the highest total score for all three grids wins.

Creating a Spinner

You'll need a paper clip and a pencil.

❶ Place one end of the paper clip over the dot at the center of the number wheel.

❷ Place the pencil point inside the paper clip on the dot.

❸ Hold the pencil firmly in place and flick the paper clip with your finger so it spins around the pencil.

❹ When the paper clip stops spinning, its tip will indicate your number.

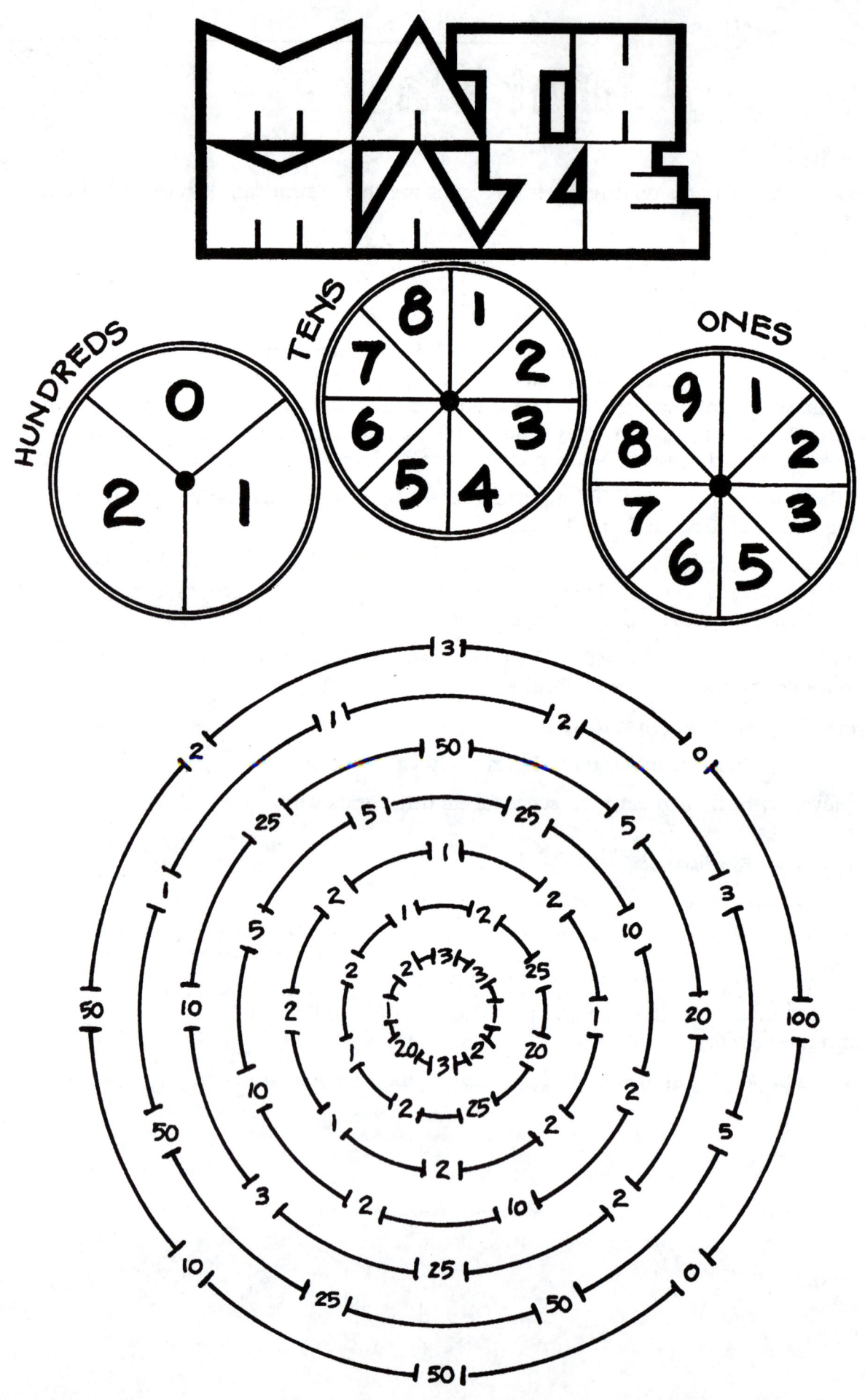

Math Maze

Objectives

✳ Reinforce place-value concepts (ones, tens, hundreds, etc.).

✳ Perform multidigit addition in your head.

Directions

❶ Each player has a copy of the "Math Maze" gameboard.

❷ The players take turns spinning all the wheels (see "Creating a Spinner" at the end of the instructions). The number Player A spins first determines the target number that both players place inside their mazes. If the spinner lands on a line, the player takes the higher number. For example, Player A spins a 6 on the ones wheel, a 3 on the tens wheel, and a 1 on the hundreds wheel. The target number that the players write inside their mazes is 136 (100 + 30 + 6).

❸ Using a pencil, each player starts anywhere outside the maze and tries to get to the center of it by adding all the numbered breaks she or he passes through. Each player can use only one numbered break from each ring and cannot skip a ring.

❹ The player who first arrives at the target number exactly wins the game. However, if neither player gets the target number exactly, the player who comes closer without exceeding it wins the game.

❺ To play another game, the players erase all their pencil marks, including the target number, and Player B spins for the new target number.

Creating a Spinner

You'll need a paper clip and a pencil.

❶ Place one end of the paper clip over the dot at the center of the number wheel.

❷ Place the pencil point inside the paper clip on the dot.

❸ Hold the pencil firmly in place and flick the paper clip with your finger so it spins around the pencil.

❹ When the paper clip stops spinning, its tip will indicate your number.

SNARE

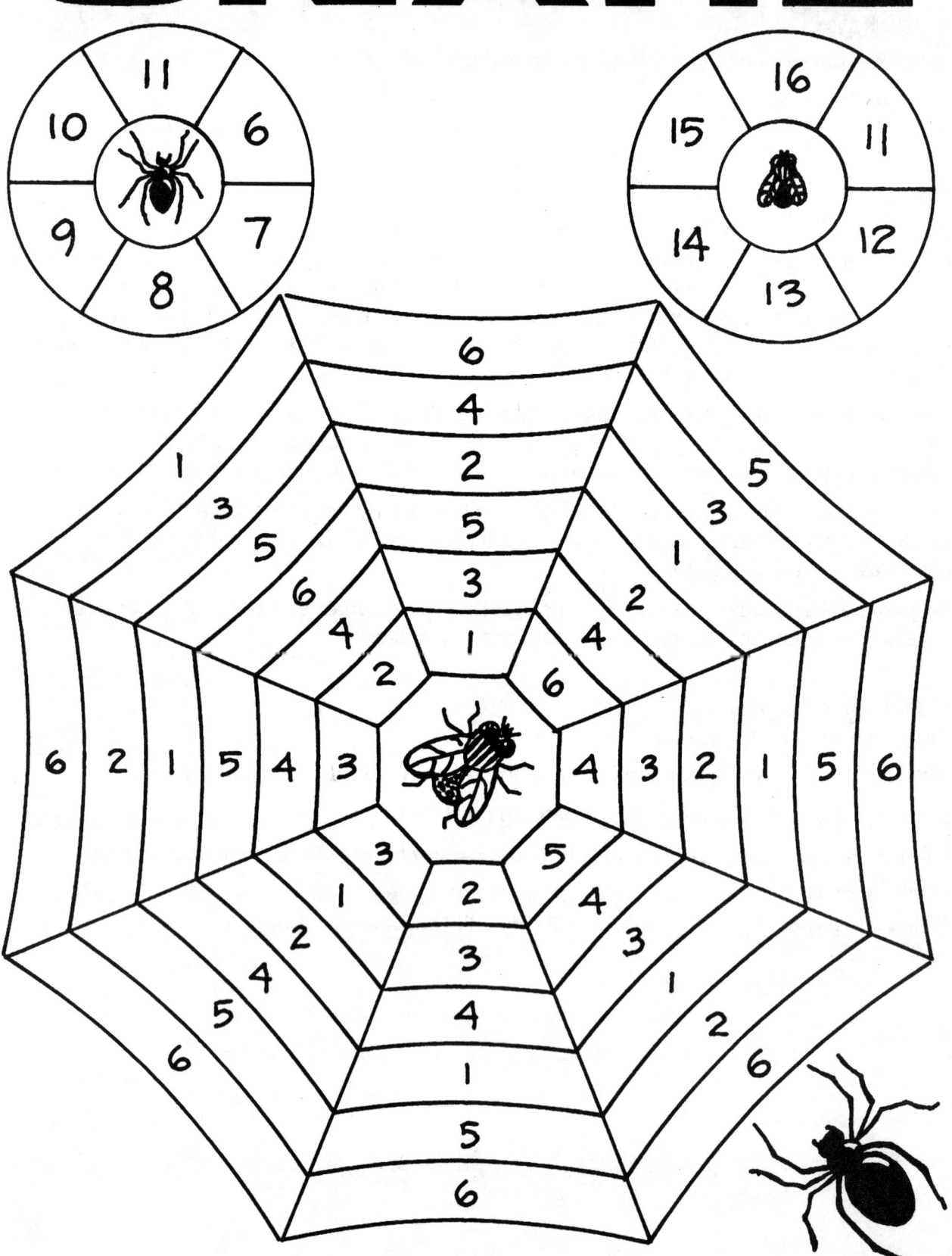

Snare

Objective
✳ Determine the addends equal to a given sum by completing a number sentence.

Directions

❶ Two players share the same "Snare" gameboard.

❷ One player is the Fly, the other is the Spider. The player who is the Fly positions a marker (chip or coin) at the center of the web on the Fly, while the player who is the Spider positions another marker outside the web on the Spider. As the game progresses, neither the Fly nor the Spider may leave the web.

❸ Each player may move in any direction on the web so long as he or she does not skip a box or pass through the center of the web. Each player may cross over any line into any touching box.

❹ The Fly always goes first. The Fly spins a number on the Fly spinner (see "Creating a Spinner" at the end of the instructions) and then moves through any touching numbered boxes to add up to that number. If, for example, the Fly spins a 15, he or she moves through any touching boxes to add up to 15. He or she may start by moving into the box marked 6 next to the Fly's position in the center of the web, and then move to the 4, 3, and 2 in the touching boxes, adding the numbers to reach 15. The Fly stops in the box with the last number added, which was 2.

❺ Trying to catch the Fly, the Spider spins on the Spider's wheel. If the player spins a 10, he or she moves the Spider marker through the touching boxes that equal 10. In this case, he or she may add 6, 2, 1, and 1 to equal 10. The Spider moves to the last number added, which was 1.

❻ If a player is unable to connect touching boxes for the number on the spinner, or if he or she adds incorrectly, the marker may not move.

❼ The Spider wins if it catches the Fly in eight or fewer moves. The Fly is caught whenever the Spider lands on the same box as the Fly. The Fly wins if it is not caught by the eighth move.

Creating a Spinner
You'll need a paper clip and a pencil.

❶ Place one end of the paper clip over the center of the number wheel.

❷ Place the pencil point inside the paper clip on the center of the wheel.

❸ Hold the pencil firmly in place and flick the paper clip with your finger so it spins around the pencil.

❹ When the paper clip stops spinning, its tip will indicate your number.

CONNECTO

(7×8) (6×9) (4×7) (3×9) (5×9)

△2×8 △9×9 △7×8 △3×6 △3×4 △5×3

(3×4) (6×8) (5×6) (7×7) (8×4)

△7×9 △8×3 △6×9 △4×5 △6×8 △8×8

(2×8) (7×9) (7×5) (3×7) (4×6)

△7×5 △0×9 △4×7 △9×6 △5×6 △7×6

(9×9) (8×3) (0×9) (6×6) (9×4)

△3×7 △6×6 △3×9 △4×4 △7×7 △4×10

(5×3) (8×8) (7×6) (4×10) (8×9)

△4×6 △9×4 △5×8 △8×7 △8×4 △8×9

(3×6) (4×5) (9×6) (4×4) (8×7)

Connecto

Objectives
✳ Perform single-digit multiplication in your head.
✳ Become familiar with the concept of continuity.

Directions

❶ Two players share the same "Connecto" gameboard. One player uses a red crayon to connect the circles, and the other player uses a blue crayon to connect the triangles.

❷ The red player tries to form a continuous path of red lines from the top row of circles to the bottom row, while the blue player tries to form a continuous path of blue lines from the left column of triangles to the right column. Lines may not cross other lines and may not run diagonally. The paths do not have to be straight; they can twist in any direction as long as they join opposite sides of the gameboard.

❸ The players take turns drawing a horizontal or vertical line between any two of their shapes, providing they can answer the problems in these shapes. They may start anywhere in their first row or column and, in turn, connect any two of their neighboring shapes on the gameboard.

❹ If a player is unable to solve the problem correctly, he or she may not draw a line. The other player then takes a turn.

❺ The player who first completes an unbroken path from one side of the gameboard to the other is the winner.

SHIP SHAPE

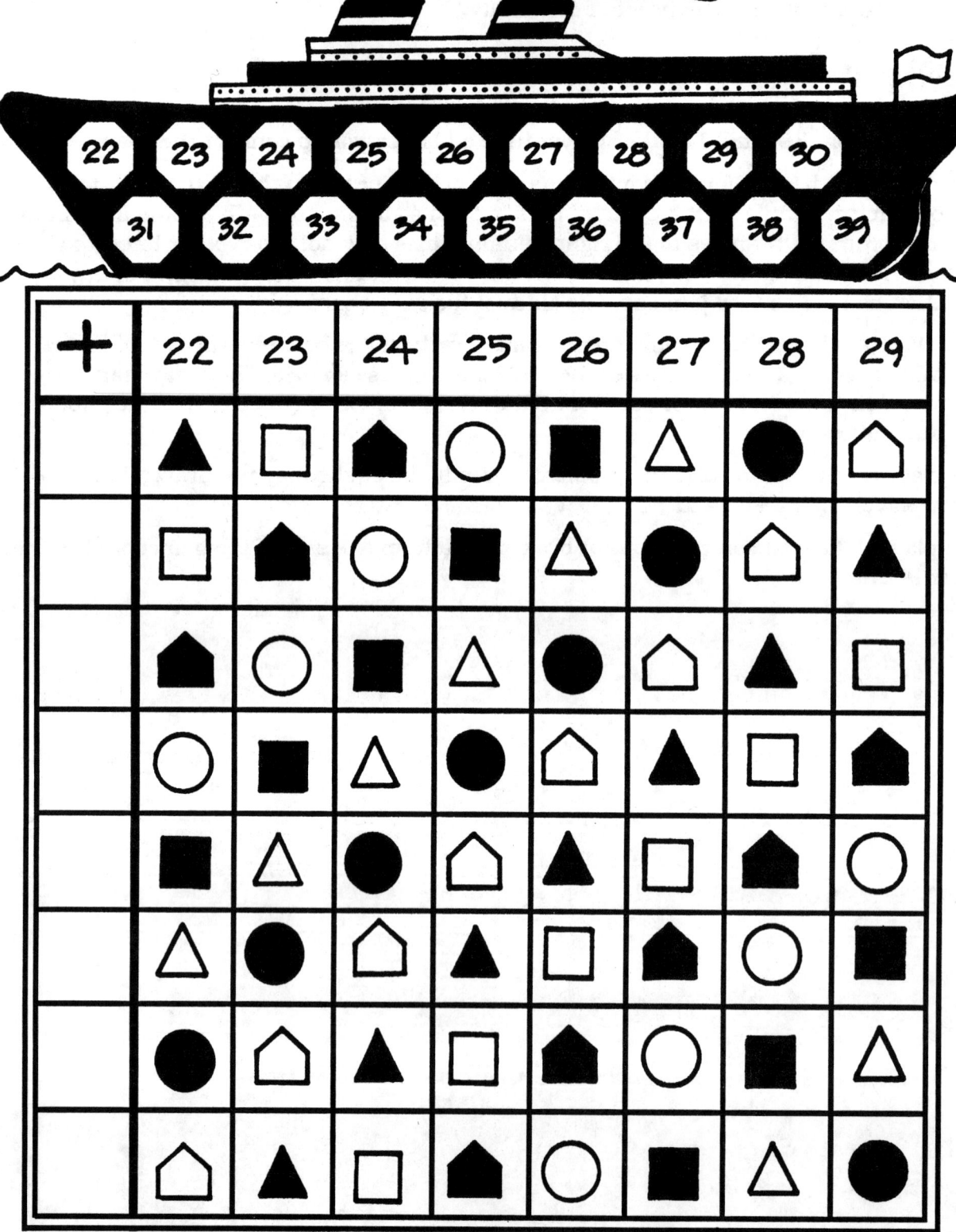

Ship Shape

Objectives

✳ Add a one-digit number to a two-digit number with and without regrouping.

✳ Learn the names and properties of geometric shapes.

Directions

❶ Each player has a copy of the "Ship Shape" gameboard.

❷ Each player chooses eight numbers from 0 to 10 and writes them in any order down the left side of the grid.

❸ In turn, each player chooses a number in one of the octagons on the ship. Both players cross out that number on the ship. Both players try to find as many different addition combinations (addends) on their grids as they can that equal the number crossed out on the ship. They place beans (or other markers) on the appropriate shapes in their grids where the two numbers to be added intersect. For example, if 28 was crossed out, and the numbers 0 through 7 were written in order down the left side of the grid, the shapes at the intersection of any of the following should be covered with a bean:

Row	Column
0	28
1	27
2	26
3	25
4	24
5	23
6	22

The row with the number 7 in it would not have a bean because there is no column with 21 in it.

❹ The players leave the beans on the grid and the second player chooses a number on the ship to cross out.

❺ Once a number on the ship has been crossed out, it cannot be reused.

❻ The player who first covers all eight of the same colored shapes (for example, eight white circles or eight black squares) wins the game.

GOOD KNIGHTS

B

3	6	2	5	4	1	7	3	6
4	7	4	1	7	5	1	8	1
7	5	8	9	3	2	4	3	9
8	3	4	2	8	3	4	7	8
7	6	5	6	4	8	2	1	2
3	5	2	9	7	6	4	3	7
2	7	3	2	5	3	8	5	2
4	1	6	2	3	7	6	2	1
8	3	4	8	5	4	7	4	5
2	5	6	3	4	3	9	1	6
4	5	6	1	8	7	3	8	2

A

Good Knights

Objectives

✸ Recognize number combinations (addends) that equal a given sum.

✸ Visualize spatial relationships that use congruent (matching) patterns.

Directions

❶ Two players share the same "Good Knights" gameboard. The players may use different-colored chess knight playing pieces or other markers.

❷ At the start of the game, one knight is positioned on the first square, ⟨3⟩ (top left), and the other is positioned on the last square, ⟨2⟩ (bottom right).

❸ The players alternate spinning the two wheels (see "Creating a Spinner" at the end of the instructions). The numbers that Player A first spins determine the target number that both players use. For example, Player A spins a 12 on Wheel I and a 5 on Wheel II and adds 12 + 5 to get 17 as the target number. If the spinner lands on a line, the higher number is used.

❹ Player A starts at the bottom right of the board and goes first. The players must move in an L-shaped pattern. An L-shaped pattern is either one space forward and two to either side, or two spaces forward and one to either side. The numbers on the four squares that make up the pattern must add up to the target number. In the example, Player A can make an L-shaped knight's move up two squares and over one. He or she adds the numbers in the four squares, 2 + 6 + 5 + 4, for a total of 17, the target number. Starting on the opposite end of the gameboard, Player B is unable to make an L-shaped move equal to 17. Player A scores 17 points; Player B scores no points.

❺ If a player adds incorrectly, he or she makes no score and does not move.

❻ Player B now spins for the new target number. Play resumes with Player A's knight marker on the ⟨4⟩ and Player B's marker remaining on the ⟨3⟩.

❼ For each turn, the players record their scores and keep running totals on scratch paper, or they may use calculators.

❽ The player whose knight is the first to reach the last row on the opposite side of the gameboard wins the game. If neither player has reached the opposite side after five spins each, the player who has scored the most points wins.

Creating a Spinner

You'll need a paper clip and a pencil.

❶ Place one end of the paper clip over the center of the number wheel.

❷ Place the pencil point inside the paper clip on the center of the wheel.

❸ Hold the pencil firmly in place and flick the paper clip with your finger so it spins around the pencil.

❹ When the paper clip stops spinning, its tip will indicate your number.